40 FRAMEWORKS
WEBDEV & APIS

An Essential Guide for Modern Developers

Diego Rodrigues

40 FRAMEWORKS WEBDev & APIs
An Essential Guide for Modern Developers

2025 Edition
Author: Diego Rodrigues
studiod21portoalegre@gmail.com

Published by StudioD21.

Important Note

The codes and scripts presented in this book aim to illustrate the concepts discussed in the chapters, serving as practical examples. These examples were developed in custom, controlled environments, and therefore there is no guarantee that they will work fully in all scenarios. It is essential to check the configurations and customizations of the environment where they will be applied to ensure their proper functioning. We thank you for your understanding.

CONTENTS

AUTHENTICATION – PROTECTION AND ACCESS MANAGEMENT

GREETINGS

Hello, dear reader!

It is with great enthusiasm that I welcome you to explore the powerful tools of web development and the versatility of APIs. Your decision to deepen your knowledge in modern frameworks reflects a remarkable commitment to professional evolution and the search for excellence in the development of efficient and scalable applications.

In this book, *"40 FRAMEWORKS WEBDev & APIs"*, you will find a complete and updated guide, covering everything from fundamental concepts to the most advanced implementations of today's most relevant frameworks. Each framework has been carefully selected to provide you with a comprehensive view of modern web development, enabling you to build robust, secure, and highly performant applications.

By dedicating yourself to this study, you are preparing yourself to face the challenges of the digital era, where speed of development, code quality and application scalability are essential. Whether you are an experienced developer looking to improve your skills or someone who wants to better understand the tools available on the market, this book will serve as a strategic roadmap to elevate your technical capabilities and allow you to make informed choices about which framework to use in each scenario.

In each chapter, we will explore a specific framework, covering its structure, functionalities, best practices and use cases. You will learn from basic concepts and installation to practical examples that demonstrate how to apply these technologies in the development of real applications. In addition, common mistakes will be presented and how to avoid them, ensuring that you are able to implement efficient and well-structured solutions from the beginning.

In a rapidly advancing digital world, mastering DevWeb frameworks and APIs is not only a competitive differentiator, but a necessity to stand out in the market. This book is designed to be a technical reference guide, allowing you to immediately apply the knowledge you have gained to creating modern, scalable applications.

Get ready for an intense and enriching journey. Each section of this book is designed to expand your skills, giving you the knowledge you need to master essential web development technologies. Together, we will explore the most innovative trends, understand how frameworks shape the way we build applications, and transform complexity into efficiency through the strategic use of the tools presented.

ABOUT THE AUTHOR
www.linkedin.com/in/diegoexpertai

Best-Selling Author, Diego Rodrigues is an International Consultant and Writer specializing in Market Intelligence, Technology and Innovation. With 42 international certifications from institutions such as IBM, Google, Microsoft, AWS, Cisco, and Boston University, Ec-Council, Palo Alto and META.

Rodrigues is an expert in Artificial Intelligence, Machine Learning, Data Science, Big Data, Blockchain, Connectivity Technologies, Ethical Hacking and Threat Intelligence.

Since 2003, Rodrigues has developed more than 200 projects for important brands in Brazil, USA and Mexico. In 2024, he consolidates himself as one of the largest new generation authors of technical books in the world, with more than 180 titles published in six languages.

BOOK PRESENTATION

Web development has never been as dynamic and essential to technological advancement as it is today. With increasingly complex applications and the growing need for scalability and security, the use of frameworks has become indispensable for optimizing the construction and maintenance of efficient systems. This book is designed to provide a structured and progressive learning experience, allowing you to master the leading DevWeb & API frameworks and make strategic choices according to your needs.

The journey begins in **Chapter 1**, with an introduction to **React**, one of the most popular frameworks for frontend development. We explore its component-based architecture, its advantages over other libraries, and how it has revolutionized the way dynamic interfaces are built. In **Chapter 2**, we move on to **Vue.js**, known for its flexibility and smooth learning curve, followed by **Angular** in **Chapter 3**, a robust framework maintained by Google and widely used in enterprise applications.

The evolution of frontend frameworks continues with **Svelte** in **Chapter 4**, which simplifies development by compiling code into highly optimized JavaScript. In **Chapter 5**, we introduce **Next.js**, a powerful React framework that enables server-side rendering and static generation. **Chapter 6** explores **Nuxt.js**, the Vue.js equivalent of Next.js, bringing developer experience improvements and SEO optimization. We conclude this module with **Chapter 7**, dedicated to **Solid.js**, an innovative framework that combines performance and reactivity in an efficient development model.

In **Module 2**, we cover backend frameworks, starting with **Express.js** in **Chapter 8**, one of the most lightweight and popular frameworks for building APIs in Node.js. In **Chapter 9**, we explore **NestJS**, which combines TypeScript and modular architecture for scalable applications. **Fastify**, in **Chapter 10**, stands out for its high performance and low resource consumption.

We then move on to Python-based frameworks with **Django** in **Chapter 11**, a comprehensive framework that provides security and productivity for web applications, followed by **Flask** in **Chapter 12**, ideal for microservices and projects requiring greater flexibility. In **Chapter 13**, we introduce **Spring Boot**, widely used in the Java community for building robust enterprise applications. In **Chapter 14**, we explore **Micronaut**, a lightweight alternative for development in Java and Kotlin, offering fast startup and low memory consumption.

Chapter 15 is dedicated to **Ruby on Rails**, known for its productivity and simplified conventions. In **Chapter 16**, we cover **Fiber**, a minimalist framework for Go that prioritizes performance and simplicity. We conclude this module with **Chapter 17**, where we explore **Laravel**, one of the most powerful and comprehensive frameworks for PHP development.

Module 3 focuses on frameworks for APIs and GraphQL, starting with **Apollo GraphQL** in **Chapter 18**, which simplifies the implementation of modern APIs. In **Chapter 19**, we introduce **Hasura**, an open-source framework that enables instant GraphQL API generation from databases. **Chapter 20** covers **GraphQL Yoga**, a lightweight and flexible option for GraphQL.

In **Chapter 21**, we explore **tRPC**, a framework that allows direct integration between frontend and backend using TypeScript. **Chapter 22** covers **LoopBack**, a framework that accelerates the creation of REST and GraphQL APIs. **Chapter 23** introduces **FastAPI**, one of the fastest frameworks for Python, ideal for building high-performance, well-documented APIs. In **Chapter 24**, we cover **Hapi.js**, a modular framework for Node.js focused on security and reliability.

Module 4 is dedicated to full-stack frameworks, starting with **RedwoodJS** in **Chapter 25**, a modern approach that combines React, GraphQL, and Prisma. In **Chapter 26**, we explore **Blitz.js**, a Rails-inspired framework designed for React and Next.js applications. **Chapter 27** introduces **AdonisJS**, a backend framework for Node.js with a robust MVC structure.

In **Chapter 28**, we cover **Meteor**, a highly integrated full-stack solution. **Chapter 29** explores **Strapi**, a flexible headless CMS for content management via APIs. We conclude the module in **Chapter 30** with **Remix**, a modern framework that leverages the power of JavaScript and hybrid rendering.

Module 5 covers frameworks for serverless and edge computing, starting with **Serverless Framework** in **Chapter 31**, which enables the construction of serverless applications with support for multiple platforms. In **Chapter 32**, we explore **Vercel**, which simplifies deploying React, Next.js, and other technologies. **Chapter 33** covers **Netlify**, a powerful solution for JAMstack application deployment and automation.

In **Chapter 34**, we introduce **AWS Amplify**, a framework for developing web and mobile applications integrated with AWS services. **Chapter 35** concludes the module with **Deno Deploy**, a platform optimized for running Deno applications in the cloud.

Finally, **Module 6** addresses security and authentication frameworks, essential for protecting applications. In **Chapter 36**, we explore **Auth.js**, a library for simplified authentication. **Chapter 37** covers **Keycloak**, a robust open-source identity and access management solution. **Chapter 38** discusses **Supabase Auth**, a modern alternative based on PostgreSQL.

Chapter 39 is dedicated to **Ory**, a framework specialized in access control. We conclude the book with **Chapter 40**, introducing **Open Policy Agent (OPA)**, a flexible mechanism for security policy management.

With this book, you will have a definitive guide to selecting and implementing the best **DevWeb & API frameworks**, whether to optimize productivity, enhance security, or develop scalable and modern applications. By mastering these tools, you will be prepared to tackle the challenges of web development and stand out in the market.

MODULE 1: FRONTEND FRAMEWORKS – BUILDING WEB INTERFACES

Frontend development has significantly evolved in recent years, driven by the need for more dynamic, high-performance, and scalable interfaces. With the increasing complexity of web applications, choosing the right framework has become essential to ensure productivity, maintainability, and an optimized user experience.

In this module, we will explore the main frontend frameworks, analyzing their features, advantages, and ideal use cases. Each of these frameworks plays a crucial role in creating modern interfaces, facilitating the implementation of reusable components, code organization, and rendering optimization.

From well-established solutions such as React, Vue.js, and Angular to innovative approaches like Svelte, Next.js, Nuxt.js, and Solid.js, this module will introduce tools that enable the development of efficient, responsive, and scalable applications. Throughout the chapters, you will learn how to install, configure, and use each framework, as well as understand best practices and avoid common mistakes.

Understanding the nuances of each technology is fundamental to making strategic decisions in building robust frontend projects. By the end of this module, you will have a solid grasp of the most relevant frameworks in the market and will be equipped to choose the ideal tool for each type of application.

CHAPTER 1 – REACT

React is a JavaScript library for building dynamic and reactive user interfaces. Created by Facebook, it allows the creation of reusable components that manage their own state and update the user interface efficiently. Its key differentiator is the adoption of the **Virtual DOM**, a mechanism that optimizes the rendering process and improves application performance by updating only the necessary elements.

The modularity of React enables developers to break down complex interfaces into small, independent, and reusable parts. This model simplifies code maintenance, making applications more scalable and organized. Additionally, React's ecosystem includes powerful libraries and tools, such as **React Router** for route management and **Redux** for advanced state control.

With a **declarative approach**, React simplifies development by allowing developers to describe how the interface should behave in different states without directly manipulating the DOM. This characteristic makes code more predictable and easier to debug, enhancing productivity and application reliability.

Installation and Basic Configuration

React can be installed in different ways, depending on the environment and project requirements. The most common method to start a new project is by using **Create React App (CRA)**, an official tool that automatically sets up the structure and initial dependencies.

To install CRA and create a new project, run:

bash

```
npx create-react-app my-project
cd my-project
npm start
```

This command creates a directory named my-project and automatically sets up a file structure, including a functional React application ready to run in the browser.

Another alternative is **Vite**, a lighter and faster tool for starting modern React projects:

bash

```
npm create vite@latest my-project --template react
cd my-project
npm install
npm run dev
```

Vite optimizes the application startup time, making it an excellent option for projects requiring higher performance during development.

Key Features and Differentiators

React stands out for several characteristics that make it a popular choice for frontend development:

- **Componentization**: Interfaces are divided into reusable components, reducing code duplication.
- **Virtual DOM**: React maintains a virtual representation of the interface in memory, comparing it with the real DOM and updating only the elements that have changed.
- **One-Way Data Binding**: Data flows in a single direction, making component behavior more predictable.
- **Hooks**: Enable the use of state and other React features

without needing class components.

- **JSX**: A syntax that combines HTML with JavaScript, simplifying interface construction.
- **Rich Ecosystem**: Support for various libraries, such as **React Router** for navigation and **Redux** for state management.

Use Cases and When to Choose It

React is ideal for applications that require interactive and reactive interfaces, such as:

- **Dynamic dashboards**: Applications that update real-time data without reloading the page.
- **Management systems (ERP, CRM)**: Environments with many reusable components and interactive forms.
- **Single-Page Applications (SPAs)**: Systems that load only one page and update content dynamically.
- **E-commerce platforms**: Interfaces requiring high interactivity and efficient loading.
- **Mobile applications**: Development of apps with **React Native**, leveraging the same React codebase.

React becomes less suitable for very simple applications that do not require a modular structure or for projects that need purely static rendering without interactivity.

Practical Demonstration with Code

The basic structure of a React component can be defined with the following implementation:

jsx

```jsx
import React, { useState } from 'react';

function Counter() {
  const [count, setCount] = useState(0);
```

```
  return (
    <div>
      <h1>Counter: {count}</h1>
      <button onClick={() => setCount(count + 1)}
>Increment</button>
    </div>
  );
}

export default Counter;
```

This code defines a functional component called Counter, which uses useState to store a numerical value and display it in the interface. The button, when clicked, increments the counter and updates the display automatically.

To use it in a React application, simply import it into the App.js file and render it within JSX:

jsx

```
import React from 'react';
import Counter from './Counter';

function App() {
  return (
    <div>
      <h1>My React Application</h1>
      <Counter />
    </div>
  );
}

export default App;
```

This modular approach makes it easy to reuse components throughout the application.

Common Errors and How to Fix Them

During React development, some common errors include:

Error: "Cannot read properties of undefined (reading 'setState')".

- **Occurs** when a state is accessed without being properly initialized or when a method is not bound to the correct context.
- **Solution**: Use useState in functional components or ensure binding in class components.

Error: "Each child in a list should have a unique 'key' prop".

- **Appears** when rendering lists without defining a unique key for each item.
- **Solution**: Always include the key property in iterated elements:

jsx

```
{items.map((item) => (
  <li key={item.id}>{item.name}</li>
))}
```

Error: "React Hook useState is called conditionally".

- **Occurs** when a hook is used inside a conditional block, violating the rule that hooks must be called in the same order in every render.
- **Solution**: Ensure that hooks are called at the top of the component function.

Best Practices and Optimization

To maintain clean, efficient, and scalable code, consider the following recommendations:

- Keep components small and specialized.
- Use hooks whenever possible, avoiding class components when unnecessary.
- Prevent unnecessary re-renders using memoization (React.memo and useMemo).
- Manage global state only when necessary, using **Context API** or libraries like **Redux**.
- Organize the project structure with a clear separation between components, services, and styles.

Alternatives and Competing Frameworks

Although React is widely used, other options offer different approaches to frontend development:

- **Vue.js**: Lighter and more intuitive, ideal for projects seeking simplicity and high performance with less configuration.
- **Angular**: A full-featured framework with **TypeScript**, recommended for robust enterprise applications requiring a structured architecture.
- **Svelte**: Eliminates the need for a virtual DOM layer, providing better performance without the complexity of traditional frameworks.
- **Solid.js**: Focused on high performance and reactivity, similar to React but with a more efficient update model.

The choice among these alternatives depends on the project requirements, the desired learning curve, and compatibility with other technologies used in the application.

Mastering React means acquiring one of the most valuable skills in modern frontend development. With a solid foundation in this framework, it is possible to build **interactive, scalable, and high-performance interfaces**, ensuring a superior experience for end users.

CHAPTER 2 – VUE.JS

Vue.js is a progressive framework for building user interfaces. Designed to be lightweight, intuitive, and highly flexible, it enables the development of dynamic web applications with an accessible learning curve. Its component-based architecture simplifies code organization and improves project maintainability, promoting an efficient development experience.

One of Vue.js's key differentiators is its **reactive approach**, which automatically updates the user interface whenever the application state changes. This feature reduces the need for direct DOM manipulation, making the code cleaner and less error-prone.

Unlike more opinionated frameworks, Vue.js can be adopted incrementally, starting as a simple library for DOM manipulation and evolving into full-fledged applications with routing and state management. Its flexibility makes it ideal for both small projects and large-scale complex systems.

Installation and Basic Configuration

Vue.js can be integrated into a project in various ways, depending on the needs and complexity of the application. The simplest method is to include Vue directly in an HTML page via **CDN**:

html

```
<!DOCTYPE html>
<html lang="en">
<head>
```

```
    <meta charset="UTF-8">
    <meta name="viewport" content="width=device-width,
initial-scale=1.0">
    <script src="https://unpkg.com/vue@3/dist/
vue.global.js"></script>
    <title>Vue.js Application</title>
</head>
<body>
  <div id="app">
    <h1>{{ message }}</h1>
  </div>

  <script>
    const app = Vue.createApp({
      data() {
        return {
          message: 'Hello, Vue.js!'
        };
      }
    }).mount('#app');
  </script>
</body>
</html>
```

This approach allows experimenting with Vue.js without requiring advanced configuration. For larger projects, the recommended method is to use **Vue CLI**, which automates configuration and optimizes project structure.

Vue CLI can be installed with the following command:

bash

```
npm install -g @vue/cli
```

```
vue create my-project
cd my-project
npm run serve
```

Alternatively, for a **faster and optimized development environment, Vite** can be used:

bash

```
npm create vite@latest my-project --template vue
cd my-project
npm install
npm run dev
```

Vite improves project load times by utilizing a more efficient development server.

Key Features and Differentiators

Vue.js stands out by offering a **balanced approach** between simplicity and performance. Some of its most relevant features include:

- **Reactive system** that automatically updates the interface when data changes.
- **Componentization** for reusable and organized code.
- **Declarative templates** that make the syntax intuitive and easy to understand.
- **Built-in directives** like v-for and v-if, simplifying DOM manipulation.
- **Simplified state management** with **Vuex** or **Pinia** for more complex applications.
- **TypeScript support**, allowing greater control over data types.
- **Incremental adaptability**, enabling seamless integration with existing projects.

Use Cases and When to Choose It

Vue.js is suitable for a wide range of applications, from **small projects** to **robust enterprise applications**. Some of the main use cases include:

- **Interactive systems** such as **admin panels and dashboards**.
- **Single-Page Applications (SPAs)** where **dynamic content updates** enhance user experience.
- **E-commerce platforms**, ensuring **interactivity and smooth navigation**.
- **Modular systems** that require **reusable components and simplified integration**.
- **Projects needing a flexible framework**, without the complexity of heavy configurations.

For applications requiring a higher level of structuring and strict development rules, Angular may be a more suitable choice.

Practical Demonstration with Code

A **Vue.js** component can be created using the Composition API or the Options API. Below is an example using the Options API, which is widely used:

html

```html
<div id="app">
  <input v-model="name" placeholder="Enter your name">
  <p>Hello, {{ name }}!</p>
</div>

<script>
const app = Vue.createApp({
  data() {
    return {
```

```
    name: "
  };
 }
}).mount('#app');
</script>
```

This code creates an interactive input field that dynamically displays the name typed by the user. The **v-model** **directive** establishes a two-way binding between the state and the input field, ensuring that any change in the input is automatically reflected in the interface.

Common Errors and How to Fix Them

During Vue.js development, some common errors include:

Error: "Property or method is not defined on the instance but referenced during render"

- **Occurs** when a variable is not defined within the data() object.
- **Solution**: Ensure all variables used in the template are correctly declared.

Error: "Avoid mutating a prop directly"

- **Appears** when **trying to modify a prop directly** passed from a parent component to a child component.
- **Solution**: Use an internal state within the child component or emit an event for the parent component to update the value.

Error: "Failed to resolve component"

- **Indicates** that a **component was not registered correctly**.
- **Solution**: Ensure the component has been properly imported and registered within the components object.

Best Practices and Optimization

To write **clean, efficient, and organized** Vue.js code, follow these best practices:

- **Break down applications into reusable components**, avoiding code duplication.
- **Use computed properties** for derived calculations, reducing unnecessary re-renders.
- **Avoid direct DOM manipulation**, preferring reactive methods for interface updates.
- **Use Vuex or Pinia** for **global state management** in larger applications.
- **Optimize component loading** with **lazy loading** and **dynamic imports**.
- **Implement accessibility best practices**, ensuring that the interface is inclusive for different users.

Alternatives and Competing Frameworks

Vue.js competes with other frontend technologies. Some of the main alternatives include:

- **React**: Popular for its flexibility and **Virtual DOM adoption**. Suitable for large-scale projects requiring an extensive range of auxiliary libraries.
- **Angular**: A **complete framework**, ideal for **enterprise applications** requiring **structured architecture** and **strict coding patterns**.
- **Svelte**: Compiles code directly into **optimized JavaScript**, eliminating the need for a **Virtual DOM**, improving performance in certain situations.

The choice between these frameworks depends on the **specific project requirements** and the **team's familiarity** with the adopted technology.

Vue.js remains one of the best options for modern frontend development due to its ease of learning, flexibility, and efficiency. Its reactive approach simplifies interface state management, making development more intuitive and productive. With an accessible learning curve and an active community, Vue.js continues to be a solid choice for developers and businesses seeking a balance between simplicity and power in building interactive interfaces.

CHAPTER 3 – ANGULAR

Angular is a frontend framework developed and maintained by Google, designed for building scalable and robust web applications. Unlike libraries such as React and Vue.js, Angular is a **complete framework**, offering a set of tools to handle routing, forms, state management, HTTP requests, and testing, without the need to install additional dependencies.

One of Angular's key differentiators is its **TypeScript-based architecture**, which provides **static typing** and **advanced features** for a more secure and organized frontend development. Additionally, Angular adopts a **dependency injection** pattern, improving modularity and code reusability.

The framework follows the **MVC (Model-View-Controller) approach** and favors the development of **highly dynamic and responsive Single-Page Applications (SPAs)**. With a well-defined lifecycle and a modular structure, Angular is widely used in enterprise applications that require **long-term maintenance, security, and scalability**.

Installation and Basic Configuration

Angular can be installed globally on the system using the **Angular CLI (Command Line Interface)**, an official tool that simplifies the creation and management of Angular projects. Installation can be done via npm:

bash

```
npm install -g @angular/cli
```

After installation, a new project can be created with the

following command:

bash

```
ng new my-angular-project
cd my-angular-project
ng serve
```

This process sets up a complete development environment with support for TypeScript, Webpack, Babel, and other essential tools. The ng serve command starts a development server, allowing real-time application visualization.

For those who prefer a **more controlled environment**, it is also possible to manually install Angular dependencies and configure the project without the CLI, but this approach is **not recommended for beginners**.

Key Features and Differentiators

Angular is a **highly structured framework**, offering various **integrated features** that optimize frontend application development. Some of its main features include:

- **Reusable components**: Its component-based architecture allows application modularization, facilitating **code reuse and maintenance**.
- **Two-Way Data Binding**: Automatically updates the **user interface** when the data model changes.
- **Dependency Injection**: Enables the creation of **loosely coupled services**, promoting **organized and testable code**.
- **Built-in Routing**: Manages navigation between different application pages **without requiring full page reloads**.
- **Reactive and Template-Driven Forms**: Two flexible approaches for **form handling and validation**.
- **Angular Universal: Server-Side Rendering (SSR)** support, improving **SEO and application load time**.

- **Lazy Loading: Dynamic module loading**, reducing application startup time.

Use Cases and When to Choose It

Angular is a recommended choice for applications that require a robust structure, security, and scalability. Some key scenarios where Angular excels include:

- **Enterprise Applications**: Corporate internal systems, dashboards, and management tools.
- **SaaS Platforms**: Applications that need **modularization and continuous maintenance**.
- **Applications with Strict Security Requirements**: With native support for **dependency injection** and **XSS protection**.
- **Long-Term Projects**: Angular's structured architecture is advantageous for applications that **need to evolve without compromising code maintainability**.

Angular may be a less suitable choice for projects requiring fast development time, as its learning curve is steeper compared to simpler frameworks like Vue.js.

Practical Demonstration with Code

The first step to **creating a component** in Angular is using the CLI:

bash

```
ng generate component my-component
```

This generates a new directory with four essential files:

- my-component.component.ts: Contains the **component logic**.
- my-component.component.html: Defines the **HTML structure**.
- my-component.component.css: Contains the **styles**

applied to the component.

- my-component.component.spec.ts: File for **automated testing**.

Below is an example of a **simple component** that displays a message and allows user interaction:

typescript

```
import { Component } from '@angular/core';

@Component({
  selector: 'app-my-component',
  template: `
    <div>
      <h2>{{ message }}</h2>
      <button (click)="changeMessage()">Change Message</
button>
    </div>
    `,
  styles: ['h2 { color: blue; }']
})
export class MyComponent {
  message: string = 'Hello, Angular!';

  changeMessage() {
    this.message = 'Message updated!';
  }
}
```

This component can be used inside the **AppComponent template** as follows:

html

```
<app-my-component></app-my-component>
```

With this structure, every time the button is clicked, the message variable will be updated, and the **interface will reflect this change**.

Common Errors and How to Fix Them

During Angular development, some common errors include:

Error: "Can't bind to 'ngModel' since it isn't a known property of 'input'."

- **Cause**: The FormsModule module was **not imported**.
- **Solution**: Add FormsModule to app.module.ts:

typescript

```
import { FormsModule } from '@angular/forms';
```

Error: "Unexpected token '<'" when loading the application.

- **Cause**: This may occur when an HTML file is interpreted as **JavaScript**.
- **Solution**: Check the angular.json configuration and ensure the **files are correctly structured**.

Error: "No provider for HttpClient!"

- **Cause**: The HttpClientModule was not **properly imported**.
- **Solution**: Include HttpClientModule in app.module.ts:

typescript

```
import { HttpClientModule } from '@angular/common/http';
```

Best Practices and Optimization

Angular offers several **optimization possibilities** to improve code efficiency and performance:

- **Use Lazy Loading** to **load modules on demand**, improving initial load time.
- **Avoid unnecessary server calls** by implementing **local caching** with **RxJS BehaviorSubject**.
- **Split the application into modules** to maintain **organized and modular code**.
- **Optimize change detection** by using **OnPush strategy** to **reduce unnecessary re-renders**.
- **Minimize global variables**, preferring **shared services** for state management.
- **Use HTTP interceptors** to handle **requests efficiently**, improving security and performance.

Alternatives and Competing Frameworks

Angular directly competes with other **popular frontend solutions**:

- **React**: A more **flexible library**, focused on **UI construction**, but **requires additional libraries** for functionalities such as **routing and state management**.
- **Vue.js**: A **lighter and more accessible framework**, ideal for **smaller projects** or those focused on **simplicity**.
- **Svelte**: An alternative that **compiles code into optimized JavaScript**, eliminating the need for **Virtual DOM**.

The choice between Angular and other technologies depends on project complexity, team familiarity, and scalability requirements.

Angular is a robust solution for large-scale frontend development. Its comprehensive ecosystem, TypeScript support, and modular architecture make it an ideal choice for enterprise applications requiring organization, security, and long-term maintainability. With efficient development practices and a structured approach, Angular remains one of the most solid options for **Single-Page Applications (SPAs)** and **complex web-based applications**.

CHAPTER 4 – SVELTE

Svelte is a reactive framework for building modern and high-performance web interfaces. Unlike other approaches such as React and Vue.js, Svelte eliminates the need for a **Virtual DOM** and compiles components directly into optimized JavaScript. This model allows applications to be **smaller, faster, and less dependent on runtime processing**.

Designed to simplify frontend development, Svelte stands out for its **intuitive syntax** and the way it handles **state and reactivity**. Instead of relying on auxiliary libraries for state management, the framework **automatically updates reactive variables** without requiring hooks or complex techniques. This approach reduces the amount of code needed to create dynamic interfaces, making development **smoother and more accessible**.

Beyond simplicity, Svelte promotes a component-based model that is encapsulated and easy to reuse. Its architecture favors writing modular and scalable code, eliminating the overhead of a heavy runtime. This concept is especially useful in applications requiring high performance, such as embedded systems, dynamic dashboards, and progressive web applications.

Installation and Basic Configuration

The recommended way to start a **Svelte project** is by using **Vite**, a lightweight tool that optimizes the development environment. To create a new project, run the following command in the terminal:

bash

```
npm create vite@latest my-project --template svelte
cd my-project
npm install
npm run dev
```

This process sets up a complete environment with Hot Module Replacement (HMR) support, ensuring that code changes are instantly reflected in the browser without needing a full page reload.

Svelte can also be used directly in an **HTML file** without requiring build tools, but this approach is **not recommended for larger projects**.

Key Features and Differentiators

Svelte offers a unique approach to frontend development, combining high performance with accessible syntax. Some of its key features include:

- **Compiles to pure JavaScript**, eliminating the need for a **Virtual DOM**.
- **Automatic reactivity**, updating the **DOM whenever the component state changes**.
- **Simple componentization**, with a structure that unifies **HTML, CSS, and JavaScript**.
- **Less code for the same functionality**, reducing complexity and development time.
- **Native support for transitions and animations**, making it easier to create **visual effects**.
- **Smaller bundle sizes**, resulting in **faster application load times**.

These features make Svelte an attractive choice for projects that require high performance without sacrificing code simplicity.

Use Cases and When to Choose It

Svelte is a recommended option for various scenarios, especially those that require high performance and reduced development complexity. Some situations where Svelte excels include:

- **Performance-focused applications**: Its **compilation model generates highly optimized code**, reducing resource consumption on the client side.
- **Lightweight interface projects**: Svelte's **simple syntax** and **lack of dependencies** make it ideal for **small and medium-sized applications**.
- **Rapid development**: The **short learning curve** allows **new developers** to quickly adopt the framework.
- **Applications requiring transitions and animations**: **Built-in support for visual effects** simplifies the creation of **interactive interfaces**.

For large-scale enterprise applications that require a well-established ecosystem, frameworks like Angular or React may be more suitable due to their extensive library support and enterprise tools.

Practical Demonstration with Code

Creating a **Svelte component** is a **straightforward process**. The **basic structure** of a component includes **HTML, CSS, and JavaScript** in the same file. A simple counter example can be built as follows:

svelte

```
<script>
  let counter = 0;

  function increment() {
    counter += 1;
```

```
  }
</script>

<style>
  button {
    background-color: #007bff;
    color: white;
    border: none;
    padding: 10px;
    cursor: pointer;
  }
</style>

<h1>Counter: {counter}</h1>
<button on:click={increment}>Increment</button>
```

The code above defines a reactive variable called counter, which automatically updates whenever the button is clicked. The on:click event calls the increment function, updating the displayed value without the need to manually manipulate the DOM.

The component can be **reused** within the application as follows:

svelte

```
<script>
  import Counter from './Counter.svelte';
</script>

<Counter />
```

This method enables modular applications with intuitive and efficient reusable components.

Common Errors and How to Fix Them

Although Svelte simplifies many aspects of frontend development, some common errors may arise during implementation:

Error: "Unexpected token '<'" when trying to run the application

- **Cause**: The **Svelte file was not compiled correctly**.
- **Solution**: Ensure the environment is correctly set up by running:

bash

```
npm install
npm run dev
```

Error: "Cannot read property 'value' of undefined"

- **Cause**: Attempting to **access an uninitialized variable**.
- **Solution**: Ensure the **variable is declared** in the component's script **before being used in the template**.

Error: "Function called outside component initialization"

- **Cause**: Attempting to **call a reactive function outside the component's scope**.
- **Solution**: Ensure **reactive values** are manipulated **within the correct scope** of the component.

Best Practices and Optimization

To ensure **clean and efficient** code, follow these best practices when using **Svelte**:

- Keep **components small and specialized**, favoring reusability.
- **Avoid excessive use of global states**, utilizing **stores only when necessary**.
- **Use reactivity only when needed**, preventing

unnecessary DOM updates.
- Take advantage of **native support for transitions and animations**, reducing external dependencies.
- **Minimize the use of global variables**, ensuring **modularity and scalability**.

Proper modularization and the adoption of best practices help maximize code efficiency, making the application more maintainable and high-performing.

Alternatives and Competing Frameworks

Svelte competes with other **popular frontend frameworks**, each with its own characteristics and ideal use cases:

- **React**: Offers **greater flexibility** and a **well-established ecosystem**, recommended for **large-scale applications** requiring **advanced state management**.
- **Vue.js**: A **balanced alternative**, with a **gentle learning curve** and a **strong community**. Suitable for applications that need **a middle ground between simplicity and structure**.
- **Angular**: The best option for **complex enterprise systems** that require **dependency injection** and **support for large development teams**.

The choice among these frameworks depends on the project's specific needs, the team size, and the long-term expectations.

Svelte stands out as one of the most innovative options for frontend development, combining simplicity, performance, and native reactivity. Its approach of eliminating the Virtual DOM and optimizing code at compile time reduces the need for heavy browser-side manipulations, making it an excellent choice for fast and efficient applications.

With a growing ecosystem and increasing adoption, Svelte continues to be a viable option for developers seeking productivity and performance in modern web development.

CAPÍTULO 5 – NEXT.JS

Next.js is a React-based frontend framework that simplifies the development of scalable and optimized web applications. Developed by Vercel, it provides advanced features for **Server-Side Rendering (SSR)**, **Static Site Generation (SSG)**, and **hybrid rendering**, allowing each page in the application to have its own loading strategy.

Unlike a traditional React application, which renders components directly in the browser, Next.js introduces a model that enhances performance, user experience, and SEO (Search Engine Optimization). By adopting techniques such as pre-rendering and optimized page loading, this framework has become a popular choice for dynamic websites, blogs, e-commerce platforms, and SaaS applications.

The Next.js architecture also simplifies routing configuration, image optimization, API support, and CDN integration, eliminating the need for manual configurations. This makes development more productive and reduces the workload required to implement caching, optimization, and infrastructure solutions.

Installation and Basic Configuration

Next.js can be quickly installed using **npm** or **yarn**. To start a new project, run the following command:

bash

```
npx create-next-app@latest my-project
cd my-project
npm run dev
```

The development server starts the application locally, allowing real-time visualization of changes.

The generated project structure includes essential directories such as:

- **pages/** – Contains the application pages, where each file automatically represents a route.
- **public/** – Stores static assets such as images and icons.
- **styles/** – Includes global styles and CSS modules.
- **api/** – A directory inside **pages/** that allows creating APIs directly within the application.

By default, Next.js includes **ESLint** and supports **TypeScript** without requiring extra configuration, making development more robust and secure.

Key Features and Differentiators

Next.js stands out for its efficient approach and integration of native functionalities that reduce frontend development complexity. Some of its key features include:

- **File-based routing** – Each file inside the **pages/** directory automatically becomes a route without manual configuration.
- **Hybrid rendering** – Supports both **SSR (Server-Side Rendering)** and **SSG (Static Site Generation)**, optimizing each page as needed.
- **Image optimization** – The **next/image** component improves image loading automatically.
- **Built-in APIs** – Allows creating **API routes** inside the **pages/api/** directory, eliminating the need for a separate backend.
- **Internationalization (i18n) support** – Simplifies the creation of multilingual applications.
- **Incremental Static Regeneration (ISR)** – Enables static page updates without requiring a full rebuild.

- **Native CSS and Tailwind CSS support** – Simplifies styling without external tools.

Use Cases and When to Choose It

Next.js is widely adopted for projects that require high performance, scalability, and SEO optimization. Some ideal applications include:

- **Blogs and institutional websites** – Uses **SSG** for fast page loading and better SEO.
- **E-commerce platforms** – Hybrid rendering to combine **static and dynamic pages**, ensuring a better user experience.
- **SaaS platforms** – Ability to create **dynamic interfaces** without sacrificing performance.
- **Enterprise applications** – Seamless integration with APIs and simplified authentication support.

For highly dynamic applications where all pages must be rendered in real-time, using React with a separate backend might be a more appropriate choice.

Practical Demonstration with Code

To create a new **Next.js page**, define a file inside the **pages/** directory. Below is an example of a homepage displaying a simple message:

jsx

```jsx
export default function Home() {
  return (
    <div>
      <h1>Welcome to Next.js!</h1>
      <p>This is a powerful framework for React.</p>
    </div>
  );
}
```

Routing is automatic, meaning this page will be directly accessible in the browser at the **/** route.

To add navigation between pages, Next.js provides the **next/ link** component, allowing **fast transitions** between routes without a full page reload:

jsx

```
import Link from 'next/link';

export default function Home() {
  return (
    <div>
      <h1>Home Page</h1>
      <Link href="/about">
        <a>Go to About Page</a>
      </Link>
    </div>
  );
}
```

The **pages/about.js** file can be created as follows:

jsx

```
export default function About() {
  return <h1>About Next.js</h1>;
}
```

Clicking the link redirects the user to the corresponding page **without reloading the entire application.**

Common Errors and How to Fix Them

Error: "Module not found: Can't resolve 'next/image'"

- **Cause**: The **next/image** package is not installed correctly.
- **Solution**: Run the following command to ensure all dependencies are updated:

bash

```
npm install next
```

Error: "Unhandled Runtime Error: 'document' is not defined"

- **Cause**: Attempting to **access document on the server**.
- **Solution**: Use useEffect to manipulate **DOM elements only on the client side**.

Error: "API resolved without sending a response"

- **Cause**: Missing **explicit response return** in an API route.
- **Solution**: Ensure the function inside **pages/api/** always returns a response using res.json().

Best Practices and Optimization

To achieve the best **performance and scalability** in Next.js applications, follow these best practices:

- Use **SSG** whenever possible for pages that **do not require dynamic rendering**.
- Leverage **ISR** to regenerate static pages **without a full rebuild**.
- Avoid **loading heavy libraries** on the client side, keeping JavaScript lightweight.
- Use **next/image** to **optimize image loading** and reduce performance impact.
- Manage global state using **Context API** or **SWR** to prevent unnecessary re-renders.
- Implement **lazy loading** for components, reducing **initial page load times**.

Alternatives and Competing Frameworks

Next.js competes with other solutions that also aim to optimize frontend development:

- **Gatsby** – Focuses on **static site generation**, making it ideal for **blogs and institutional websites**.
- **Remix** – Provides a **hybrid rendering model** similar to Next.js but with a different approach to **data fetching**.
- **Nuxt.js** – A Vue.js alternative offering **similar functionalities** for Vue-based applications.

Choosing between these frameworks depends on project requirements, library support, and the adopted rendering model.

Next.js is a powerful solution for React applications that require performance optimization and flexible rendering. Its hybrid rendering support, automatic optimizations, and seamless API integration make it a strategic choice for modern web development.

By applying best practices and exploring its native features, developers can build scalable, efficient applications that meet the demands of the digital market.

CHAPTER 6 – NUXT.JS

Nuxt.js is a Vue.js-based framework designed to facilitate the creation of modern, scalable, and optimized web applications. It offers a flexible approach to page rendering, allowing developers to choose between SSR (Server-Side Rendering), SSG (Static Site Generation), and hybrid rendering. This makes Nuxt.js ideal for applications requiring high performance, improved SEO, and optimized loading.

Unlike a traditional Vue.js project, which executes all processing on the client side, Nuxt.js enables **pre-rendering** pages on the server before sending them to the browser. This significantly reduces initial load time and improves indexing by search engines, making it an efficient solution for blogs, e-commerce sites, and dynamic platforms.

In addition to its advanced rendering model, Nuxt.js provides a structured architecture that improves code organization and reduces the need for manual configurations. With built-in support for automatic routing, incremental page loading, and API integration, the framework eliminates configuration complexity, allowing developers to focus on application development.

Installation and Basic Configuration

Nuxt.js can be quickly installed using **create-nuxt-app**, which generates an optimized development structure:

bash

```
npx nuxi init my-project
cd my-project
```

```
npm install
npm run dev
```

This command sets up a complete development environment, including support for TypeScript, ESLint, Tailwind CSS, and PWA, depending on the choices made during the initial configuration.

The project structure includes essential directories:

- **pages/** – Defines application routes automatically.
- **components/** – Stores reusable components.
- **layouts/** – Defines global layouts for pages.
- **static/** – Contains static files such as images and fonts.
- **plugins/** – Stores third-party library extensions.

Automatic routing eliminates the need for manual route configuration, simplifying navigation between pages.

Key Features and Differentiators

Nuxt.js offers a set of advanced features that optimize both development and user experience:

- **Hybrid rendering** – Supports SSR, SSG, and incremental page generation, allowing optimization based on application needs.
- **Automatic routing** – Each file inside the **pages/** directory automatically becomes an accessible route.
- **Enhanced SEO** – Pre-rendering pages on the server improves indexing and load times.
- **State management** – Native integration with **Pinia** for global application state control.
- **Image optimization** – Native support for optimized image loading, reducing bandwidth consumption.
- **Middleware support** – Enables authentication and access control rules for pages and routes.
- **Internationalization (i18n) support** – Simplified configuration for multilingual applications.

These features make Nuxt.js a complete frontend solution, eliminating the need for external dependencies for advanced optimizations.

Use Cases and When to Choose It

Nuxt.js is ideal for applications requiring optimized performance and good search engine indexing. Some key scenarios include:

- **Blogs and institutional websites** – Benefit from **SSG** for fast loading and improved SEO.
- **E-commerce platforms** – Hybrid rendering optimizes both static and dynamic product pages.
- **Dashboards and SaaS platforms** – The **modular organization** of Nuxt.js facilitates the creation of **complex and scalable applications**.
- **Authentication-based systems** – Built-in **middleware** allows easy route protection and access management.

For highly dynamic applications where all pages are rendered in real-time without SEO requirements, traditional Vue.js may be a lighter alternative.

Practical Demonstration with Code

Creating a **page in Nuxt.js** is simple. Just add a file inside the **pages/** directory. A basic example of a homepage can be structured as follows:

vue

```
<template>
  <div>
    <h1>Welcome to Nuxt.js!</h1>
    <p>This is a powerful framework for Vue.js.</p>
  </div>
</template>
```

This file will automatically be accessible at the **/** route.

To create a link between pages, the **NuxtLink** component is used:

vue

```
<template>
  <div>
    <h1>Home Page</h1>
    <NuxtLink to="/about">Go to About Page</NuxtLink>
  </div>
</template>
```

The **pages/about.vue** file can be added as follows:

vue

```
<template>
  <div>
    <h1>About Nuxt.js</h1>
    <p>A framework for Vue.js with optimized rendering.</p>
  </div>
</template>
```

With this structure, Nuxt.js **automatically manages routing**, ensuring smooth transitions between pages.

Common Errors and How to Fix Them

Error: "Cannot find module '@nuxt/types'"

- **Cause**: Essential dependencies are missing.
- **Solution**: Run the following command to ensure all required packages are installed:

bash

npm install

Error: "NuxtServerError: Request failed with status code 500"

- **Cause**: Middleware issues or failed asynchronous requests.
- **Solution**: Check server logs and ensure all API calls return valid responses.

Error: "Invalid prop type: Expected String, got Number"

- **Cause**: Incorrect data type passed to a component.
- **Solution**: Ensure all data types are correctly defined and validated in the Vue component.

Best Practices and Optimization

To achieve better performance and organization when using Nuxt.js, follow these best practices:

- Use **nuxt generate** to **pre-render static pages** whenever possible, reducing server load.
- Take advantage of **lazy loading** to **dynamically load components**, preventing unnecessary code execution.
- Implement **data caching** with useAsyncData to **avoid redundant API requests**.
- Maintain a **modular structure** by separating **components, pages, and layouts**, ensuring scalability.
- Utilize **middleware** for authentication control, preventing unnecessary loading of protected pages.

These practices help maximize **application performance and maintainability**.

Alternatives and Competing Frameworks

Nuxt.js competes with other optimized frontend rendering solutions, such as:

- **Next.js** – A React-based framework with a similar SSR and SSG approach, ideal for React-optimized projects.
- **Gatsby** – Focused on **static site generation**, better suited for **content-driven** websites and **advanced SEO**.
- **VuePress** – A solution designed for **documentation and technical blogs**, built on Vue.js.

Choosing between these options depends on the **technology stack** used and the level of control required over application rendering.

Nuxt.js is an efficient solution for optimized Vue.js applications, combining flexibility, performance, and ease of use. With support for hybrid rendering, automatic routing, and built-in SEO tools, the framework stands out as a strategic option for developers seeking a balance between productivity and performance.

By applying best practices and leveraging its native features, it is possible to build fast, scalable applications ready for the demands of the digital market.

CHAPTER 7 – SOLID.JS

Solid.js is a reactive framework for web interface development that stands out for its innovative approach, eliminating the need for a **Virtual DOM** and offering extremely efficient reactivity. Its execution model is based on signals and effects, allowing state updates to be immediately reflected in the DOM without unnecessary re-renders.

With support **for JSX and an intuitive syntax, Solid.js becomes a powerful choice for developers already familiar with React** but looking for better performance and lower resource consumption. It is especially useful for applications requiring intense reactivity, such as interactive dashboards and Single Page Applications (SPAs).

Installation and Basic Configuration

Solid.js can be quickly installed using npx degit to create a new project with Vite:

sh

```
npx degit solidjs/templates my-solid-app
cd my-solid-app
npm install
npm run dev
```

To add Solid.js to an existing project, simply run:

sh

```
npm install solid-js
```

Solid.js works best with Vite, ensuring fast builds and automatic optimizations.

Key Features and Differentiators

- Reactivity without Virtual DOM, eliminating the overhead of element reconciliation.
- Signals (createSignal) and effects (createEffect) allow precise control over DOM updates.
- Efficient rendering without the need for diffing or complex calculations.
- Modular componentization, making code organization and element reuse easier.
- Native support for SSR (Server-Side Rendering) and SSG (Static Site Generation), optimizing SEO and initial loading.

Use Cases and When to Choose It

Solid.js is ideal for projects requiring high reactivity and performance, such as:

- **Administrative panels and dashboards**, where multiple states need real-time updates.
- **Single Page Applications (SPAs)**, ensuring smooth user interaction.
- **Applications where performance is critical**, eliminating unnecessary re-renders.
- **Reusable components within high-performance frontend ecosystems**.

If extreme reactivity and lower memory consumption are priorities, Solid.js stands out as a highly optimized solution.

Practical Demonstration with Code

Below is a reactive counter using createSignal:

jsx

```
import { createSignal } from "solid-js";

function Counter() {
  const [count, setCount] = createSignal(0);

  return (
    <div>
      <p>Current value: {count()}</p>
      <button onClick={() => setCount(count() + 1)}
>Increment</button>
      <button onClick={() => setCount(count() - 1)}
>Decrement</button>
    </div>
  );
}

export default Counter;
```

Here, the state is stored as a signal (createSignal), ensuring instant reactivity without the need for Virtual DOM reconciliation.

Common Errors and How to Fix Them

Error: "Function count is not a function"

- **Cause**: Attempting to access a signal (createSignal) as a direct value instead of calling it as a function.
- **Solution**: Always call signals as functions when accessing them.

Incorrect:

jsx

```jsx
<p>{count}</p>
```

Correct:

jsx

```jsx
<p>{count()}</p>
```

Error: "Cannot assign to read-only property 'count'"

- **Cause**: Trying to modify a signal directly instead of using setCount.
- **Solution**: Always use the signal update function.

Incorrect:

jsx

```jsx
count = count() + 1;
```

Correct:

jsx

```jsx
setCount(count() + 1);
```

Error: "SolidJS Hooks must be called at the top level"

- **Cause**: Calling createSignal or createEffect inside loops, conditionals, or nested functions.
- **Solution**: Ensure hooks are called at the top level of the component function.

Incorrect:

jsx

```
if (condition) {
  const [count, setCount] = createSignal(0);
}
```

Correct:

jsx

```
const [count, setCount] = createSignal(0);
if (condition) {
  console.log(count());
}
```

Best Practices and Optimization

- Use createSignal for mutable states, ensuring efficient change tracking.
- Avoid unnecessary calls to setCount to prevent excessive re-renders.
- Use createMemo() for derived calculations, reducing redundant processing.
- Keep state logic separate from visual components, ensuring modularity.
- Use onCleanup() within effects (createEffect) to prevent memory leaks.

Alternatives and Competing Frameworks

Solid.js positions itself as a high-performance competitor against popular frameworks:

- **React.js** – Solid.js offers superior reactivity and a more efficient update model without needing a Virtual DOM.

- **Vue.js** – While Vue has a robust reactivity system, Solid.js eliminates the need for proxies and manual tracking.
- **Svelte** – Both compile optimized code, but Solid.js maintains full JSX compatibility and better control over reactivity.

Each technology has its benefits, but Solid.js excels in applications demanding maximum efficiency and optimized rendering.

Solid.js represents an innovative approach to frontend development, ensuring faster reactive interfaces, lower memory consumption, and a superior user experience. With its signal-based reactivity and highly efficient rendering, it becomes an excellent choice for developers prioritizing performance and fluidity in web development.

MODULE 2: BACKEND FRAMEWORKS – SERVERS AND WEB APPLICATIONS

The backend is the backbone of any modern web application, responsible for data processing, security, authentication, database communication, and providing APIs for the frontend. In this module, we explore the main backend frameworks, their characteristics, and applications, helping in the selection of the best tool for different development scenarios.

Throughout the chapters, we will cover frameworks developed in different programming languages, such as Node.js, Python, Java, Ruby, Go, and PHP, providing a broad view of the available options. Each framework offers a unique approach to building servers and applications, ranging from minimalist solutions to full-featured frameworks that provide a structured environment for large corporate systems.

Key topics covered in this module include:

- The difference between minimalist and full-stack frameworks, and when each should be used.
- How to choose the best framework for a project, considering scalability, performance, security, and maintainability.
- The impact of the programming language on framework selection, considering compatibility with other tools and services.
- Optimization strategies and best practices in backend development, ensuring efficient, secure, and

maintainable code.

Popular frameworks such as Express.js, Django, Spring Boot, and Laravel will be explored in detail, along with emerging alternatives such as Fastify, Micronaut, and Fiber, which offer high performance and lower resource consumption.

By the end of this module, it will be possible to understand the advantages and challenges of each framework, enabling strategic decision-making when developing robust and scalable servers and web applications.

CAPÍTULO 8 – EXPRESS.JS (NODE.JS)

Express.js is a minimalist framework for building servers and web applications using Node.js. It provides a lightweight layer over the Node.js core, simplifying the development of APIs and scalable applications. Unlike more structured frameworks, Express.js maintains a flexible approach, allowing developers to choose their own strategies for code organization, request handling, and middleware management.

The main advantage of Express.js is its simplicity. It offers an efficient router, middleware support, and easy integration with databases and other libraries. This lightweight and modular design makes Express.js the predominant choice for developing REST APIs, microservices, and real-time applications.

In addition to being widely adopted in backend applications, Express.js serves as the foundation for more advanced frameworks such as NestJS, Fastify, and Sails.js, reinforcing its importance within the Node.js ecosystem.

Installation and Basic Configuration

Installing Express.js requires Node.js and a package manager such as npm or yarn. To start a new project, the first step is to create a directory and initialize the project:

bash

```
mkdir my-project
cd my-project
```

```
npm init -y
```

Next, Express.js can be installed with the following command:

bash

```
npm install express
```

Once installed, a basic server can be quickly created. The code below starts an Express.js server that responds with "Hello, world!" on the main route:

javascript

```javascript
const express = require('express');
const app = express();
const port = 3000;

app.get('/', (req, res) => {
  res.send('Hello, world!');
});

app.listen(port, () => {
  console.log(`Server running at http://localhost:${port}`);
});
```

Running this code with node index.js will start the server on port 3000, ready to process requests.

Key Features and Differentiators

Express.js stands out for its simplicity and flexibility, allowing developers to configure the backend as they prefer. Some of its most important features include:

- **Flexible routing** – Allows the creation of dynamic and modular HTTP routes.

- **Middleware support** – Facilitates request processing before reaching the routes.
- **Native JSON support** – Efficiently handles data sent by REST APIs.
- **Database integration** – Compatible with MongoDB, PostgreSQL, MySQL, and other technologies.
- **Asynchronous execution** – Leverages Node.js's event-driven model for greater scalability.
- **WebSocket support** – Enables real-time application development with Socket.io.

Express.js is highly extensible and allows developers to choose libraries for authentication, caching, security, and file handling without imposing a fixed structure.

Use Cases and When to Choose It

Express.js is an excellent choice for projects that require a fast, flexible, and scalable backend. Some of its main use cases include:

- **RESTful APIs** – Developing efficient and optimized APIs for integration with frontend and mobile systems.
- **Microservices** – A distributed architecture that allows modular scalability.
- **Real-time applications** – Chat systems, notifications, and data streaming.
- **API gateways** – Intermediating services and standardizing communication between applications.
- **Backends for web applications** – Integrating with databases, authentication, and business logic.

For applications requiring a highly structured code model, **NestJS** may be a more suitable alternative, as it adds architectural patterns on top of Express.js.

Practical Demonstration with Code

Express.js allows for the efficient creation of REST APIs. Below is an example of an API for managing a To-Do List with CRUD (Create, Read, Update, Delete) operations:

javascript

```javascript
const express = require('express');
const app = express();
const port = 3000;

app.use(express.json());

let tasks = [
  { id: 1, title: 'Study Express.js', completed: false },
  { id: 2, title: 'Create REST API', completed: false }
];

// List all tasks
app.get('/tasks', (req, res) => {
  res.json(tasks);
});

// Create a new task
app.post('/tasks', (req, res) => {
  const newTask = {
    id: tasks.length + 1,
    title: req.body.title,
    completed: false
  };
  tasks.push(newTask);
  res.status(201).json(newTask);
});

// Update a task
app.put('/tasks/:id', (req, res) => {
```

```
const task = tasks.find(t => t.id === parseInt(req.params.id));
if (!task) return res.status(404).json({ message: 'Task not
found' });

task.title = req.body.title || task.title;
task.completed = req.body.completed !== undefined ?
req.body.completed : task.completed;

res.json(task);
});

// Delete a task
app.delete('/tasks/:id', (req, res) => {
tasks = tasks.filter(t => t.id !== parseInt(req.params.id));
res.status(204).send();
});

app.listen(port, () => {
console.log(`Server running at http://localhost:${port}`);
});
```

This API provides endpoints to list, add, update, and delete tasks, demonstrating the flexibility and simplicity of Express.js for backend service development.

Common Errors and How to Fix Them

Error: "Cannot GET /route"

- **Cause**: The route is not properly defined.
- **Solution**: Ensure the route path is correctly declared in the code.

Error: "req.body is undefined"

- **Cause**: Missing middleware for parsing JSON in Express.js.

- **Solution**: Add app.use(express.json()); before defining the routes.

Error: "Address already in use"

- **Cause**: The server port is already in use.
- **Solution**: Change the port number in the code or terminate the process using the port.

Best Practices and Optimization

To ensure that an Express.js application is **scalable and secure**, follow these best practices:

- Use **middlewares for input validation**, preventing invalid or malicious data.
- Implement **authentication and authorization** using JWT or OAuth.
- **Handle errors globally**, ensuring standardized responses for unexpected failures.
- Use a **logging framework** such as Morgan or Winston for application monitoring.
- Configure **caching** to optimize frequent requests using Redis or similar solutions.

Alternatives and Competing Frameworks

Although Express.js is one of the most popular backend development options for Node.js, other alternatives can be considered:

- **Fastify** – A faster, high-performance framework with lower resource consumption.
- **NestJS** – Adds a more structured and modular framework over Express.js, using robust architectural patterns.
- **Koa** – Created by the same developers as Express.js, offering greater flexibility with fewer internal dependencies.

Express.js remains the default choice for backend development with Node.js, combining simplicity, flexibility, and an active community. Its widespread adoption and extensive compatibility with libraries make it one of the most versatile frameworks for creating scalable servers and APIs. By applying best practices and proper optimization, it is possible to develop robust and highly performant systems.

CHAPTER 9 – NESTJS (NODE.JS)

NestJS is a backend **framework for Node.js that combines modular architecture, TypeScript, and Angular-inspired design patterns.** It is designed to provide a robust structure for building scalable APIs, microservices, and enterprise applications, making code maintenance and organization easier.

Unlike minimalist frameworks such as Express.js and Fastify, NestJS follows an opinionated approach, promoting a more structured and modular codebase. Its dependency injection system and native TypeScript support help create more secure, organized, and testable applications.

With an architecture based on the Model-View-Controller (MVC) pattern and influenced by Angular, NestJS simplifies the creation of controllers, services, and reusable modules, fostering separation of concerns and scalability. Its compatibility with Express.js and Fastify libraries makes it flexible, allowing developers to optimize for high performance or better request control.

Installation and Basic Configuration

To start a NestJS project, the first step is to install the CLI (Command Line Interface), which simplifies project creation and management:

bash

```
npm install -g @nestjs/cli
```

With the CLI installed, a new project can be generated using the following command:

bash

```
nest new my-project
cd my-project
npm run start
```

The default NestJS structure includes:

- **src/** – Main application directory
- **app.module.ts** – Defines application modules and dependencies
- **app.controller.ts** – Controller managing routes and responses
- **app.service.ts** – Service for business logic and data processing
- **main.ts** – Application entry file where the server is initialized

The code below demonstrates a basic server in NestJS:

typescript

```
import { NestFactory } from '@nestjs/core';
import { AppModule } from './app.module';

async function bootstrap() {
  const app = await NestFactory.create(AppModule);
  await app.listen(3000);
  console.log('Server running at http://localhost:3000');
}

bootstrap();
```

With this structure, the NestJS server will be ready to handle incoming requests.

Key Features and Differentiators

NestJS stands out by offering native tools for structured and scalable backend development. Some of its most important features include:

- **Modular architecture** – Organizes applications into modules, facilitating code reuse.
- **TypeScript support** – Enhances security and improves the development experience.
- **Dependency injection** – Simplifies component decoupling and maintenance.
- **Microservices support** – Compatible with RabbitMQ, Kafka, gRPC, and other protocols.
- **Middleware and interceptors** – Provides advanced control over requests and responses.
- **Integrated ORM support** – Works with Prisma, TypeORM, Mongoose, and Sequelize.
- **Authentication and security** – Built-in support for JWT, OAuth, and session-based authentication.

These features make NestJS ideal for projects requiring a clear structure, security, and scalability, avoiding the complexity of unstructured architectures.

Use Cases and When to Choose It

NestJS is recommended for backend projects that require high organization and modularity. Some of the main use cases include:

- **REST APIs and GraphQL** – Applications needing well-structured and scalable endpoints.
- **Microservices and distributed architecture** – Implementation of asynchronous service communication.
- **Enterprise platforms** – Internal systems requiring security and best architectural practices.

- **API gateways** – Integration between multiple backend services.
- **Real-time applications** – WebSockets for notifications and live chat.

NestJS may be a better choice than Express.js when long-term maintainability, modular organization, and extensive TypeScript usage are required.

Practical Demonstration with Code

Creating a REST API with NestJS follows an organized structure. A controller can be created to manage routes as follows:

typescript

```
import { Controller, Get } from '@nestjs/common';

@Controller('tasks')
export class TasksController {
  @Get()
  getTasks() {
    return [{ id: 1, title: 'Learn NestJS', completed: false }];
  }
}
```

This code defines a controller that responds to GET requests on the **/tasks** route. To make it work, it needs to be registered inside a module:

typescript

```
import { Module } from '@nestjs/common';
import { TasksController } from './tasks.controller';

@Module({
```

```
  controllers: [TasksController],
})
export class TasksModule {}
```

The module must then be imported into **app.module.ts** to ensure the controller is properly loaded into the application.

To add a service that separates business logic, the structure can be organized as follows:

typescript

```
import { Injectable } from '@nestjs/common';

@Injectable()
export class TasksService {
  private tasks = [{ id: 1, title: 'Learn NestJS', completed: false }];

  getTasks() {
    return this.tasks;
  }
}
```

The controller can be modified to use the service:

typescript

```
import { Controller, Get } from '@nestjs/common';
import { TasksService } from './tasks.service';

@Controller('tasks')
export class TasksController {
  constructor(private readonly tasksService: TasksService) {}

  @Get()
  getTasks() {
```

```
    return this.tasksService.getTasks();
  }
}
```

This separation between controllers, services, and modules improves organization, scalability, and maintainability.

Common Errors and How to Fix Them

Error: "Cannot find module '@nestjs/common'"

- **Cause**: NestJS dependencies were not installed properly.
- **Solution**: Run the following command to ensure all required dependencies are installed:

bash
```
npm install
```

Error: "Nest can't resolve dependencies"

- **Cause**: A service or controller was not registered in the corresponding module.
- **Solution**: Check if the services and controllers are properly declared in their modules.

Error: "404 Not Found when accessing route"

- **Cause**: The controller is not being loaded correctly.
- **Solution**: Ensure the controller is imported and registered in the main module.

Best Practices and Optimization

To keep a NestJS application efficient, follow these best practices:

- Use **modules** to organize the code, dividing functionalities into independent parts.
- Properly **inject dependencies** to ensure low coupling between services.

- Implement **authentication and security**, using JWT or OAuth.
- Take advantage of **TypeScript's strong typing** to prevent errors and improve code robustness.
- Configure **input validation with class-validator** to prevent invalid data from being processed.
- **Monitor and log system activity** to facilitate debugging and performance analysis.

Alternatives and Competing Frameworks

NestJS competes directly with other Node.js backend development solutions:

- **Express.js** – A minimalist alternative for smaller and more flexible projects.
- **Fastify** – A high-performance option with lower resource consumption.
- **Koa** – Created by the same developers as Express.js but designed with a more modern and lightweight approach.

NestJS stands out as the best option for applications requiring modular organization, scalability, and native TypeScript support. Its structured approach allows the development of robust and secure APIs, making it easier to build enterprise projects and distributed architectures. By applying best practices and leveraging its built-in features, developers can create efficient and highly scalable backend systems.

CHAPTER 10 – FASTIFY (NODE.JS)

Fastify is a **minimalist and high-performance backend framework for Node.js,** designed to offer high speed, security, and low resource consumption. It stands out for being faster than Express.js and for implementing a plugin-based architecture with native JSON Schema validation, ensuring efficient request processing.

Unlike heavier frameworks, Fastify prioritizes low overhead and modularity, making it an ideal choice for RESTful APIs, microservices, and cloud applications. Its structure facilitates code reuse, allowing developers to build scalable backend applications without sacrificing simplicity.

Another key feature of Fastify is its built-in logging system, which improves debugging and performance analysis. With native support for TypeScript, GraphQL, and input validation, it caters to both small projects and complex systems that require high request throughput.

Installation and Basic Configuration

To start using Fastify, Node.js must be installed, and a new project must be initialized. The first step is to set up a working environment:

bash

```
mkdir my-project
cd my-project
npm init -y
```

Then, Fastify can be installed with:

bash

```
npm install fastify
```

Once installed, a basic server can be quickly created:

javascript

```javascript
const fastify = require('fastify')({ logger: true });

fastify.get('/', async (request, reply) => {
  return { message: 'Hello, Fastify!' };
});

fastify.listen({ port: 3000 }, (err, address) => {
  if (err) {
    fastify.log.error(err);
    process.exit(1);
  }
  console.log(`Server running at ${address}`);
});
```

This code initializes a server on port 3000, automatically logging each request. Fastify handles asynchronous responses natively, making the backend more efficient.

Key Features and Differentiators

Fastify was developed to overcome the limitations of older frameworks, providing a set of functionalities that optimize performance and security:

- **Low resource consumption** – Designed to handle thousands of simultaneous requests without overloading the CPU.

- **Automatic validation with JSON Schema** – Reduces the need for external libraries to validate data.
- **Plugin system** – Allows applications to be extended in a modular and reusable way.
- **Native TypeScript support** – Ensures better code security and predictability.
- **Built-in logging with Pino** – Logs events and errors efficiently, improving debugging.
- **Optimized middleware** – Reduces latency and improves response times.
- **Express.js compatibility** – Allows developers to migrate applications without major changes.

These differentiators make Fastify an efficient alternative for modern backend applications, especially those requiring optimized performance and high scalability.

Use Cases and When to Choose It

Fastify is recommended for projects that require high performance and low latency. Some of its main use cases include:

- **High-performance APIs** – Applications that handle a large volume of requests per second.
- **Microservices** – Distributed architectures that need fast communication between services.
- **Real-time applications** – Systems requiring quick responses, such as notifications and data streaming.
- **API gateways** – Middleware solutions connecting clients to multiple backend services.
- **Serverless backends** – Integration with platforms like AWS Lambda and Google Cloud Functions.

For applications that require more structured architectures and an MVC pattern, frameworks like NestJS may be a better choice.

Practical Demonstration with Code

Fastify enables the creation of REST APIs in an optimized manner, ensuring that each request is processed with minimal overhead. Below is an example of a CRUD API for user management:

javascript

```javascript
const fastify = require('fastify')({ logger: true });

let users = [
  { id: 1, name: 'Alice' },
  { id: 2, name: 'Bob' }
];

// List users
fastify.get('/users', async (request, reply) => {
  return users;
});

// Create a new user
fastify.post('/users', async (request, reply) => {
  const newUser = { id: users.length + 1, ...request.body };
  users.push(newUser);
  reply.status(201).send(newUser);
});

// Update user
fastify.put('/users/:id', async (request, reply) => {
  const { id } = request.params;
  const user = users.find(u => u.id === parseInt(id));
  if (!user) {
    return reply.status(404).send({ message: 'User not found' });
```

```
  }

  Object.assign(user, request.body);
  reply.send(user);
});

// Delete user
fastify.delete('/users/:id', async (request, reply) => {
  users = users.filter(u => u.id !==
parseInt(request.params.id));
  reply.status(204).send();
});

fastify.listen({ port: 3000 }, (err, address) => {
  if (err) {
    fastify.log.error(err);
    process.exit(1);
  }
  console.log(`Server running at ${address}`);
});
```

This API allows listing, adding, updating, and removing users, demonstrating how Fastify simplifies backend development without losing efficiency.

Common Errors and How to Fix Them

Error: "Cannot find module 'fastify'"

- **Cause**: Fastify was not installed correctly.
- **Solution**: Run the following command to ensure Fastify is installed:

bash

```
npm install fastify
```

Error: "Cannot read property 'body' of undefined"

- **Cause**: The server was not configured to process JSON.
- **Solution**: Add Fastify's form body parser:

javascript

```
fastify.register(require('@fastify/formbody'));
```

Error: "Address already in use"

- **Cause**: The server port is already being used by another process.
- **Solution**: Change the port in the code or terminate the process occupying it.

Best Practices and Optimization

Fastify is already optimized by default, but some additional practices can help maintain application performance:

- **Use plugins** to modularize features, improving code organization.
- **Implement caching** to reduce repetitive requests using Redis or a similar solution.
- **Enable detailed logging** for performance monitoring.
- **Avoid blocking async execution**, ensuring operations do not obstruct request processing.
- **Validate input with JSON Schema** to prevent data injection attacks and unexpected errors.

Alternatives and Competing Frameworks

Fastify competes directly with other Node.js backend solutions, each with its own characteristics:

- **Express.js** – The most popular and flexible framework, but less optimized for high performance.
- **NestJS** – A modular TypeScript-based architecture, ideal

for large and structured projects.

- **Koa** – Created by the same developers as Express.js, offering a more lightweight and modern approach.

Fastify stands out as the best option for applications requiring high performance without losing simplicity. Its low resource consumption, native JSON Schema support, and efficient logging system make it one of the fastest frameworks for modern APIs. By applying best practices and leveraging its advanced features, developers can build scalable and efficient backends ready for large-scale applications.

CHAPTER 11 – DJANGO (PYTHON)

Django is a full-stack web framework for Python, designed to enable fast, secure, and scalable backend development. Created under the "batteries included" philosophy, it provides a complete set of built-in tools, including database management, authentication, templating system, and advanced security features.

Unlike minimalist frameworks like Flask, Django enforces an organized structure based on the **MTV (Model-Template-View)** pattern, which facilitates the separation of business logic, presentation layer, and data handling. Its ORM (Object-Relational Mapping) system simplifies database interactions, allowing developers to manipulate data using Python without writing SQL manually.

Another key advantage of **Django is its focus on security and scalability**, offering protection against common attacks such as SQL Injection, Cross-Site Scripting (XSS), and Cross-Site Request Forgery (CSRF), making it a reliable choice for enterprise applications and large-scale platforms.

Installation and Basic Configuration

To start a project with Django, the framework must be installed, and a virtual environment should be configured to isolate the project. The first step is to create a virtual environment using Python:

bash

```
python -m venv venv
```

```
source venv/bin/activate   # On Windows, use: venv\Scripts
\activate
```

With the virtual environment activated, install Django with:

bash

```
pip install django
```

After installation, create a new project with:

bash

```
django-admin startproject my_project
cd my_project
python manage.py runserver
```

The server will start on port 8000, and the project structure will include essential files such as:

- manage.py – Command-line tool for managing the project.
- settings.py – Django configuration file, including database, security, and middleware settings.
- urls.py – Defines the application's routes.
- views.py – Controllers that handle HTTP requests.
- models.py – Defines the database tables.

To create a new application within the project, use:

bash

```
python manage.py startapp my_app
```

This modular structure facilitates project organization and scalability.

Key Features and Differentiators

Django stands out for its comprehensive and structured approach, eliminating the need for external libraries for essential features. Some of its main features include:

- **Integrated ORM** – Enables database manipulation without writing SQL queries.
- **Built-in authentication system** – Supports login, permissions, and security mechanisms.
- **Automatic administration interface** – Provides a ready-to-use interface for managing data.
- **Advanced security** – Includes protections against XSS, CSRF, and SQL Injection.
- **Template system** – Separates business logic from presentation.
- **Customizable middleware** – Allows advanced request and response handling.
- **REST API support** – Seamless integration with Django REST Framework for scalable API development.

These features make Django a strong choice for building secure and efficient backend applications while reducing development time.

Use Cases and When to Choose It

Django is widely used in projects that require high productivity and security. Some of its main use cases include:

- **E-commerce platforms** – Manages products, payments, and user accounts efficiently.
- **Enterprise systems** – Suitable for applications with complex business logic and multiple users.
- **Scalable REST APIs** – Enables data services for frontend applications and mobile devices.
- **News portals and blogs** – Supports dynamic content generation with a built-in admin interface.
- **SaaS applications** – Handles multi-client support with authentication and role management.

For smaller applications or those requiring more architectural flexibility, Flask may be a lighter alternative.

Practical Demonstration with Code

To create a simple task management API with Django, start by defining the data model in models.py:

python

```
from django.db import models

class Task(models.Model):
    title = models.CharField(max_length=200)
    completed = models.BooleanField(default=False)

    def __str__(self):
        return self.title
```

After defining the model, update the database with:

bash

```
python manage.py makemigrations
python manage.py migrate
```

Next, create a controller to handle requests in views.py:

python

```
from django.http import JsonResponse
from .models import Task

def list_tasks(request):
    tasks = list(Task.objects.values())
    return JsonResponse({'tasks': tasks})
```

To associate this function with a route, configure urls.py:

python

```
from django.urls import path
from .views import list_tasks

urlpatterns = [
    path('tasks/', list_tasks),
]
```

By accessing http://localhost:8000/tasks/, the API will return the list of registered tasks in the database.

Common Errors and How to Fix Them

Error: "ModuleNotFoundError: No module named 'django'"

- **Cause**: Django is not installed in the virtual environment.
- **Solution**: Activate the virtual environment and run:

bash

```
pip install django
```

Error: "ProgrammingError: relation 'task' does not exist"

- **Cause**: Database migrations were not applied correctly.
- **Solution**: Run:

bash

```
python manage.py migrate
```

Error: "CSRF verification failed"

- **Cause**: A POST request was sent without a valid CSRF

token.

- **Solution**: Add @csrf_exempt to the view decorator or properly configure form submissions.

Best Practices and Optimization

To maintain an efficient and secure Django project, consider the following best practices:

- **Modularize code by separating logic into apps** – Create independent apps to maintain clean architecture.
- **Use token-based authentication** – Implement JWT for secure API authentication.
- **Enable caching** – Configure Redis or Memcached to reduce database load.
- **Maintain error logs** – Use Sentry or Django Logging to track application issues.
- **Use environment variables** – Avoid exposing sensitive information in the source code.
- **Disable DEBUG mode in production** – Prevent sensitive data from being leaked.

Following these practices ensures that applications remain scalable, secure, and maintainable.

Alternatives and Competing Frameworks

Django competes with other Python web frameworks and backend solutions, each with its own strengths:

- **Flask** – A minimalist framework that provides more flexibility for small projects.
- **FastAPI** – Focused on high performance with native support for asynchronous APIs.
- **Express.js (Node.js)** – A lightweight alternative for JavaScript-based backend applications.
- **Spring Boot (Java)** – Suitable for enterprise-grade systems requiring high scalability.

Django remains one of the best choices for structured backend development, combining security, productivity, and a mature ecosystem. Its opinionated and feature-complete approach allows developers to build robust applications quickly without relying on multiple third-party tools. By applying best practices and leveraging Django's advanced features, it is possible to create scalable, secure, and production-ready systems.

CAPÍTULO 12 – FLASK (PYTHON)

Flask is a microframework for Python, known for its simplicity and flexibility. Designed for agile development, Flask provides only the essentials for building web applications, leaving developers the freedom to choose libraries and extensions according to project needs.

Unlike full-stack frameworks such as Django, Flask does not impose a rigid architectural model, allowing each application to be structured in a customized way. Its minimalist approach makes it ideal for RESTful APIs, microservices, and lightweight web applications, where simplicity and granular control over components are essential.

Despite being lightweight, Flask has a large community and a robust ecosystem of extensions, enabling the addition of ORM support, authentication, caching, security, and session management without compromising the framework's flexibility.

Installation and Basic Configuration

Flask can be installed quickly using pip, Python's package manager. To maintain an isolated environment, it is recommended to create a virtual environment before installation:

bash

```
python -m venv venv
source venv/bin/activate # On Windows, use: venv\Scripts\activate
```

With the environment activated, install Flask with:

bash

```
pip install flask
```

After installation, a basic server can be started with the following code:

python

```
from flask import Flask

app = Flask(__name__)

@app.route('/')
def home():
    return 'Hello, Flask!'

if __name__ == '__main__':
    app.run(debug=True)
```

Running the script will start the server on port 5000, allowing access to the main route at http://127.0.0.1:5000/.

Key Features and Differentiators

Flask stands out for its simplicity and modularity, enabling the creation of lightweight applications without the need for complex configurations. Its key features include:

- **Flexible routing** – Simple configuration of routes and request handling.
- **Customizable middleware** – Easily extend functionalities without modifying the application core.
- **Template support with Jinja2** – Enables dynamic rendering of HTML pages.

- **Built-in session management** – Simplifies user authentication and control.
- **JSON and REST API support** – Facilitates the development of web services for frontend and mobile integration.
- **Compatibility with various libraries** – Easy integration with SQLAlchemy, Marshmallow, Flask-Login, and other extensions.

This lightweight and modular approach makes Flask an excellent choice for projects requiring flexibility and rapid development.

Use Cases and When to Choose It

Flask is widely used in projects that do not require the complexity of full-stack frameworks. Some key scenarios where it excels include:

- **RESTful APIs** – Efficient and scalable web service development.
- **Microservices** – Implementation of small, independent applications within distributed architectures.
- **Lightweight web applications** – Development of admin panels, dashboards, and internal tools.
- **Rapid prototyping** – Building MVPs (Minimum Viable Products) and validating ideas before scaling a project.
- **API gateways** – Acting as an intermediary between clients and backend services.

For applications requiring a complete structure, integrated administration, and advanced security, Django may be a more robust option.

Practical Demonstration with Code

Creating a simple REST API using Flask can be done with Flask-RESTful, an extension that adds native support for HTTP methods and data serialization. The following code demonstrates a task management service:

python

```python
from flask import Flask, jsonify, request

app = Flask(__name__)

tasks = [
    {'id': 1, 'title': 'Learn Flask', 'completed': False},
    {'id': 2, 'title': 'Create REST API', 'completed': False}
]

@app.route('/tasks', methods=['GET'])
def list_tasks():
    return jsonify(tasks)

@app.route('/tasks', methods=['POST'])
def create_task():
    new_task = {
        'id': len(tasks) + 1,
        'title': request.json['title'],
        'completed': False
    }
    tasks.append(new_task)
    return jsonify(new_task), 201

@app.route('/tasks/<int:id>', methods=['PUT'])
def update_task(id):
    task = next((t for t in tasks if t['id'] == id), None)
    if task is None:
        return jsonify({'error': 'Task not found'}), 404

    task['title'] = request.json.get('title', task['title'])
```

```
    task['completed'] = request.json.get('completed',
task['completed'])
    return jsonify(task)

@app.route('/tasks/<int:id>', methods=['DELETE'])
def delete_task(id):
    global tasks
    tasks = [t for t in tasks if t['id'] != id]
    return '', 204

if __name__ == '__main__':
    app.run(debug=True)
```

This API allows listing, adding, updating, and deleting tasks, demonstrating how Flask simplifies backend development.

Common Errors and How to Fix Them

Error: "ImportError: No module named flask"

- **Cause**: Flask is not installed, or the virtual environment is not activated.
- **Solution**: Run pip install flask and ensure the virtual environment is activated correctly.

Error: "KeyError: 'title'" when sending a POST request

- **Cause**: The JSON request does not contain the expected field.
- **Solution**: Ensure that the request body includes a valid JSON payload.

Error: "Address already in use"

- **Cause**: Another instance of the server is running on the same port.
- **Solution**: Stop the running process or change the port using app.run(port=5001).

Best Practices and Optimization

To keep a Flask application efficient and scalable, some best practices should be followed:

- **Use Blueprints** – Modularize the code by dividing functionalities into different files.
- **Implement secure authentication** – Use JWT or OAuth for access control.
- **Enable caching** – Configure Redis to reduce database queries.
- **Set up detailed logging** – Use the logging library to track errors and critical events.
- **Avoid running in production with** debug=True – Use a production-ready server such as Gunicorn.

These practices ensure that the application remains secure, scalable, and easy to maintain.

Alternatives and Competing Frameworks

Flask competes with other Python web frameworks, each with specific characteristics:

- **Django** – A full-stack solution with built-in administration and higher security.
- **FastAPI** – Optimized for performance and native support for asynchronous APIs.
- **Tornado** – Focused on real-time applications and persistent connections.

Flask remains one of the best options for agile backend development, providing a balance between simplicity and power. Its minimalist approach allows developers to create fast APIs and modular, scalable systems, ensuring productivity without sacrificing flexibility. By applying best practices and leveraging Flask's extensions, developers can build efficient and scalable applications, ready for future growth.

CHAPTER 13 – SPRING BOOT (JAVA)

Spring Boot is a backend framework for Java designed to **simplify the development** of robust, scalable, and production-ready applications. It extends the Spring Framework, offering a set of tools and conventions that eliminate much of the manual configuration required for traditional Java projects.

The key differentiator of Spring Boot is its **"opinionated"** approach, which defines best practices and standards for developing REST APIs, microservices, and enterprise applications. It allows projects to be initialized quickly, with minimal configuration and native support for databases, security, caching, messaging, and monitoring.

With modular architecture support, dependency injection, and integration with modern technologies such as Docker and Kubernetes, Spring Boot has become the standard choice for scalable cloud systems and corporate applications.

Installation and Basic Configuration

The most practical way to start a Spring Boot project is by using **Spring Initializr**, a tool that automatically generates the project's initial structure. Access Spring Initializr and configure:

- **Language**: Java
- **Project type**: Maven or Gradle
- **Dependencies**: Spring Web, Spring Boot DevTools, and Spring Data JPA (for database integration)

After downloading the generated project, run the application with:

bash

```
mvn spring-boot:run  # For Maven projects
gradle bootRun       # For Gradle projects
```

The initial project structure includes:

- **Application.java** – The main class that starts the Spring Boot server.
- **Controller.java** – Controllers responsible for handling HTTP requests.
- **Service.java** – The business logic layer of the application.
- **Repository.java** – Interface for database communication.

To test the installation, a simple controller can be created:

java

```
import org.springframework.web.bind.annotation.GetMapping;
import org.springframework.web.bind.annotation.RequestMapping;
import org.springframework.web.bind.annotation.RestController;

@RestController
@RequestMapping("/api")
public class HelloController {

    @GetMapping("/hello")
    public String hello() {
        return "Hello, Spring Boot!";
    }
}
```

Running the application makes the route **http://localhost:8080/api/hello** available.

Key Features and Differentiators

Spring Boot stands out by offering a comprehensive set of features that simplify backend development:

- **Quick startup** – Applications can be created without requiring manual configuration.
- **Embedded server** – Uses Tomcat, Jetty, or Undertow without external setup.
- **Dependency injection** – Based on the Spring Framework, allowing modular and reusable applications.
- **Native database integration** – Supports JPA, Hibernate, and JDBC for efficient SQL and NoSQL database communication.
- **Microservices support** – Enables the development of scalable, distributed applications using Spring Cloud.
- **Monitoring and metrics** – Tools like Actuator provide real-time application performance monitoring.
- **Advanced authentication and security** – Spring Security offers protection against attacks such as XSS, CSRF, and SQL Injection.

With these features, Spring Boot enables the development of scalable REST APIs, integrations with messaging systems (Kafka, RabbitMQ), and resilient applications for production environments.

Use Cases and When to Choose It

Spring Boot is widely adopted in enterprise projects and large-scale applications. Key use cases include:

- **REST APIs and microservices** – Efficient communication between distributed services.
- **E-commerce platforms** – Order management, payments,

and secure user control.

- **Corporate systems and ERP** – Managing internal processes and integrating with complex databases.
- **Cloud applications** – Integration with Kubernetes and support for horizontal scalability.
- **Financial and banking applications** – Compliance with security standards for sensitive transactions.

For smaller applications or those requiring lower resource consumption, frameworks like **Quarkus** or **Micronaut** may be more efficient.

Practical Demonstration with Code

A complete REST API in Spring Boot follows a model based on **Controller, Service, and Repository**, ensuring separation of concerns.

Creating an Entity Model

The first step is to define an entity for data persistence. In **Tarefa.java**:

java

```java
import jakarta.persistence.*;

@Entity
@Table(name = "tarefas")
public class Tarefa {

    @Id
    @GeneratedValue(strategy = GenerationType.IDENTITY)
    private Long id;

    private String titulo;
    private boolean concluida;

    // Getters and Setters
```

}

Creating a Repository for Database Access

The **TarefaRepository.java** interface allows data manipulation without writing SQL manually:

java

```java
import
org.springframework.data.jpa.repository.JpaRepository;

public interface TarefaRepository extends
JpaRepository<Tarefa, Long> {
}
```

Creating a Service for Business Logic

The service encapsulates the rules for handling tasks in **TarefaService.java**:

java

```java
import org.springframework.stereotype.Service;
import java.util.List;

@Service
public class TarefaService {

    private final TarefaRepository repository;

    public TarefaService(TarefaRepository repository) {
        this.repository = repository;
    }

    public List<Tarefa> listarTodas() {
        return repository.findAll();
```

```
    }

    public Tarefa salvar(Tarefa tarefa) {
        return repository.save(tarefa);
    }
}
```

Creating a REST Controller

Finally, a controller is created in **TarefaController.java** to expose the endpoints:

java

```java
import org.springframework.web.bind.annotation.*;

import java.util.List;

@RestController
@RequestMapping("/api/tarefas")
public class TarefaController {

    private final TarefaService service;

    public TarefaController(TarefaService service) {
        this.service = service;
    }

    @GetMapping
    public List<Tarefa> listarTarefas() {
        return service.listarTodas();
    }

    @PostMapping
    public Tarefa criarTarefa(@RequestBody Tarefa tarefa) {
```

```
    return service.salvar(tarefa);
  }
}
```

With this structure, the API is available at the following endpoints:

- **GET /api/tarefas** – Returns all tasks.
- **POST /api/tarefas** – Creates a new task in the database.

Common Errors and How to Fix Them

Error: "Field tarefaRepository required a bean of type 'TarefaRepository' that could not be found"

- **Cause**: The **TarefaRepository** interface is not correctly registered.
- **Solution**: Ensure that the @Repository annotation or inheritance from JpaRepository is configured.

Error: "No identifier specified for entity"

- **Cause**: The entity class does not have a field annotated with @Id.
- **Solution**: Ensure that there is a unique identifier in the entity with @GeneratedValue(strategy = GenerationType.IDENTITY).

Error: "Database connection refused"

- **Cause**: Incorrect database configuration in application.properties.
- **Solution**: Check if the database is running and if the credentials are correct.

Best Practices and Optimization

To ensure an efficient and scalable application with Spring Boot, the following best practices should be adopted:

- **Use profiles for different environments** (application-dev.properties, application-prod.properties).

- **Enable caching** to optimize frequent queries using Redis or Caffeine.
- **Configure logging** with Logback or SLF4J to track failures and critical events.
- **Use DTOs (Data Transfer Objects)** to avoid direct exposure of entities.
- **Implement pagination** to prevent massive data returns in public APIs.

Spring Boot remains the most consolidated solution for modern Java applications, combining performance, modularity, and native scalability support. By applying best practices and leveraging its advanced features, it is possible to develop resilient, secure, and production-ready systems.

CHAPTER 14 –
MICRONAUT (JAVA)

Micronaut is a modern framework for developing microservices and cloud-native applications in Java, Kotlin, and Groovy. Designed to overcome the limitations of traditional frameworks, it focuses on low memory consumption, fast startup, and compatibility with serverless environments.

Unlike frameworks such as Spring Boot, which use reflection and dynamic proxies for dependency injection, Micronaut performs class analysis at compile time, drastically reducing startup time and resource usage. This makes it an ideal choice for high-performance APIs, reactive applications, and scalable microservices.

With native support for gRPC, HTTP, reactive databases, JWT authentication, distributed monitoring, and integration with Kubernetes and AWS Lambda, Micronaut positions itself as an efficient alternative for developers needing an optimized framework prepared for modern architectures.

Installation and Basic Configuration

Micronaut can be installed via the **Micronaut CLI**, **Maven**, or **Gradle**. To install the CLI, use the following command:

bash

```
sdk install micronaut
```

After installation, create a new project with:

bash

```
mn create-app com.example.myapp --build=maven --lang=java
cd myapp
./mvnw clean install
./mvnw mn:run
```

The server will start on port **8080**, ready to receive requests.

The generated project structure includes:

- **Application.java** – The main class that initializes the Micronaut server.
- **Controller.java** – Handles HTTP requests.
- **Service.java** – Business logic layer.
- **Repository.java** – Interface for database communication.

To create a basic controller, add the following:

java

```java
import io.micronaut.http.annotation.Controller;
import io.micronaut.http.annotation.Get;

@Controller("/api")
public class HelloController {

    @Get("/hello")
    public String hello() {
        return "Hello, Micronaut!";
    }
}
```

The API will now be available at **http://localhost:8080/api/hello**.

Key Features and Differentiators

Micronaut offers a set of features that make it an efficient solution for microservices and reactive applications. Some of its main features include:

- **Compile-time dependency injection** – Reduces application startup time.
- **Low memory consumption** – Ideal for execution in containers and serverless architectures.
- **Asynchronous and reactive APIs** – Compatible with RxJava, Project Reactor, and Kotlin Coroutines.
- **Native authentication with JWT** – Built-in support for OAuth 2.0 and OpenID Connect.
- **Distributed configuration** – Integration with Consul, Eureka, and Kubernetes.
- **Monitoring and distributed tracing** – Compatible with Zipkin and Jaeger for request tracing.
- **GraalVM support** – Allows compiling applications into native images, further reducing startup time.

These characteristics make Micronaut an ideal solution for cloud-native development and optimized execution in high-concurrency environments.

Use Cases and When to Choose It

Micronaut excels in projects requiring low latency, fast startup, and scalable microservices support. Some ideal applications include:

- **High-performance REST APIs** – Backend services requiring efficiency and scalability.
- **Microservices in distributed environments** – Applications running in **Kubernetes** or **service mesh** architectures.
- **Serverless applications** – Execution in **AWS Lambda, Google Cloud Functions, and Azure Functions**.

- **Messaging services** – Integration with **RabbitMQ, Kafka, and MQTT** for asynchronous communication.
- **Financial and telecommunications systems** – Processing high volumes of real-time data.

For projects requiring a mature codebase and a larger community, Spring Boot may be a more consolidated alternative.

Practical Demonstration with Code

A **REST API** for task management can be created using **Controller, Service, and Repository**, ensuring separation of concerns.

Creating an Entity Model

In **Tarefa.java**, define the entity to be stored in the database:

java

```java
import io.micronaut.data.annotation.*;
import io.micronaut.data.model.*;

import javax.persistence.*;

@Entity
@Table(name = "tarefas")
public class Tarefa {

    @Id
    @GeneratedValue
    private Long id;

    private String titulo;
    private boolean concluida;

    // Getters and Setters
```

```
}
```

Creating a Repository for Database Access

The **TarefaRepository.java** interface allows data manipulation without writing SQL manually:

java

```java
import io.micronaut.data.annotation.Repository;
import io.micronaut.data.jpa.repository.JpaRepository;

@Repository
public interface TarefaRepository extends
JpaRepository<Tarefa, Long> {
}
```

Creating a Service for Business Logic

The service encapsulates the task manipulation rules in **TarefaService.java**:

java

```java
import jakarta.inject.Singleton;
import java.util.List;

@Singleton
public class TarefaService {

    private final TarefaRepository repository;

    public TarefaService(TarefaRepository repository) {
        this.repository = repository;
    }

    public List<Tarefa> listarTodas() {
```

```java
    return repository.findAll();
}

public Tarefa salvar(Tarefa tarefa) {
    return repository.save(tarefa);
}
}
```

Creating a REST Controller

The **TarefaController.java** exposes the endpoints for task management:

java

```java
import io.micronaut.http.annotation.*;
import java.util.List;

@Controller("/api/tarefas")
public class TarefaController {

    private final TarefaService service;

    public TarefaController(TarefaService service) {
        this.service = service;
    }

    @Get
    public List<Tarefa> listarTarefas() {
        return service.listarTodas();
    }

    @Post
    public Tarefa criarTarefa(@Body Tarefa tarefa) {
        return service.salvar(tarefa);
```

```
    }
}
```

The API will be available at the following endpoints:

- **GET /api/tarefas** – Returns all tasks.
- **POST /api/tarefas** – Creates a new task in the database.

Common Errors and How to Fix Them

Error: "No such bean of type 'TarefaRepository'"

- **Cause**: The repository is not correctly registered.
- **Solution**: Ensure the @Repository annotation is present in the repository interface.

Error: "Unsupported Media Type: application/json" when sending a POST request

- **Cause**: The request was not sent correctly with JSON.
- **Solution**: Ensure that the Content-Type: application/json header is included in the request.

Error: "Database connection refused"

- **Cause**: Incorrect database configuration.
- **Solution**: Verify credentials and configurations in application.yml.

Best Practices and Optimization

To ensure an **efficient and scalable** application with Micronaut, adopt the following practices:

- **Use GraalVM** to reduce startup time and memory consumption.
- **Implement caching** to optimize frequent queries using **Caffeine** or **Redis**.
- **Configure structured logs** for efficient application monitoring.
- **Utilize distributed tracing support** to monitor requests in distributed systems.

- **Enable security with JWT** for user authentication.

Micronaut establishes itself as one of the best options for cloud-native development, offering superior performance, modular architecture, and compatibility with distributed environments. By applying best practices and leveraging its advanced features, it is possible to develop lightweight, efficient, and production-ready microservices.

CAPÍTULO 15 – RUBY ON RAILS (RUBY)

Ruby on Rails, often referred to simply as Rails, is a full-stack web development framework for Ruby, known for its simplicity, productivity, and emphasis on convention over configuration. Designed to accelerate application development, Rails enables the creation of APIs and complete applications with less code and a structured approach.

The core concept of Rails is **"Convention over Configuration,"** which establishes standards that eliminate the need for extensive configurations. This allows developers to build functional applications quickly without manually defining every aspect of the environment.

Another fundamental principle of Rails is **"Don't Repeat Yourself" (DRY),** which encourages code reuse and modular organization, resulting in more maintainable and scalable applications. With built-in support for **ORM (Active Record), routing, templates, authentication, and security,** Rails has become one of the most popular solutions for startups, SaaS applications, and enterprise projects.

Installation and Basic Configuration

Rails requires **Ruby** and the **RubyGems** package manager to be installed. To install Rails globally, use the following command:

bash

```
gem install rails
```

After installation, create a new project with:

bash

```
rails new my_application
cd my_application
rails server
```

This initializes a local server on **port 3000**, allowing access to the application at **http://localhost:3000**.

The generated project structure includes:

- **app/** – Contains controllers, models, and views.
- **config/** – Configuration files for the application.
- **db/** – Database structure and migrations.
- **routes.rb** – Defines the application's routes.

To create a basic controller, run:

bash

```
rails generate controller Home index
```

This creates a **home_controller.rb** file with an **index** method, accessible at **http://localhost:3000/home/index**.

Key Features and Differentiators

Rails is a comprehensive solution for web development, providing a robust set of tools for building scalable and secure applications. Some of its key features include:

- **Active Record (native ORM):** Simplifies database manipulation without requiring manual SQL queries.
- **Code autogeneration:** Automatically creates controllers, models, and migrations.
- **Intuitive routing system:** Defines URLs in a simple and

structured manner.

- **RESTful API support:** Enables the creation of services for frontend and mobile integrations.
- **Built-in security:** Protection against XSS, CSRF, and SQL Injection.
- **Automated testing tools:** Supports test-driven development (TDD/BDD).
- **Scaffold generation:** Quickly creates complete CRUD functionalities.

These features make Rails one of the most productive choices for developers seeking a complete and efficient framework.

Use Cases and When to Choose It

Rails is widely used in startups, SaaS applications, and projects requiring **rapid implementation and scalability**. Some of its primary use cases include:

- **E-commerce systems:** Fast development of online stores.
- **SaaS platforms:** Multi-user applications for online services.
- **REST APIs for frontend applications:** Integration with **React, Vue.js, and other modern frameworks**.
- **Content management platforms (CMSs):** Dynamic websites and admin dashboards.
- **Community portals and social networks:** High-traffic collaborative applications.

For projects requiring low latency and ultra-fast startup times, lightweight frameworks such as Sinatra may be more efficient.

Practical Demonstration with Code

A REST API for task management in Rails follows the Model-View-Controller (MVC) pattern.

Creating the Data Model

The first step is to generate a **Task** model with the required attributes:

bash

```
rails generate model Task title:string completed:boolean
rails db:migrate
```

This creates the **tasks** table in the database.

Creating a Controller for Task Management

The **tasks_controller.rb** file is automatically created with the following command:

bash

```
rails generate controller Tasks
```

In **app/controllers/tasks_controller.rb**, define the methods to manage tasks:

ruby

```
class TasksController < ApplicationController

  def index
    tasks = Task.all
    render json: tasks
  end

  def create
    task = Task.new(task_params)
    if task.save
      render json: task, status: :created
    else
      render json: task.errors, status: :unprocessable_entity
    end
```

```ruby
  end

  def update
    task = Task.find(params[:id])
    if task.update(task_params)
      render json: task
    else
      render json: task.errors, status: :unprocessable_entity
    end
  end

  def destroy
    task = Task.find(params[:id])
    task.destroy
    head :no_content
  end

  private

  def task_params
    params.require(:task).permit(:title, :completed)
  end

end
```

Configuring Routes

Define API routes in **config/routes.rb**:

ruby

```ruby
Rails.application.routes.draw do
  resources :tasks
end
```

This configuration automatically creates the following endpoints:

- **GET /tasks** – Lists all tasks.
- **POST /tasks** – Creates a new task.
- **PUT /tasks/:id** – Updates an existing task.
- **DELETE /tasks/:id** – Removes a task from the database.

Common Errors and How to Fix Them

Error: "Could not find a JavaScript runtime" when running Rails

- **Cause:** Rails requires a JavaScript runtime for compiling assets.
- **Solution:** Install **Node.js** and **Yarn** with:

bash

```
brew install node yarn
```

Error: "ActiveRecord::PendingMigrationError" when starting the server

- **Cause:** Database migrations have not been applied.
- **Solution:** Run:

bash

```
rails db:migrate
```

Error: "No route matches" when accessing a route

- **Cause:** The route has not been correctly defined.
- **Solution:** Verify **config/routes.rb** and run:

bash

rails routes

to check available routes.

Best Practices and Optimization

To ensure an efficient and scalable **Rails** application, follow these best practices:

- **Use caching:** Enable caching to reduce repeated database queries.
- **Optimize SQL queries:** Use **select, includes, and joins** to prevent unnecessary queries.
- **Configure environment variables:** Use **dotenv** to store credentials securely.
- **Implement secure authentication:** Use **Devise or JWT** for access control.
- **Monitor the application:** Use tools like **New Relic or Skylight** to track performance.

Alternatives and Competing Frameworks

Rails directly competes with other full-stack and minimalist frameworks:

- **Sinatra (Ruby):** A lightweight alternative for small APIs.
- **Django (Python):** A full-featured framework for structured applications.
- **Spring Boot (Java):** A robust option for **scalable enterprise applications**.
- **Express.js (Node.js):** A minimalist framework for backend development in JavaScript.

Rails remains one of the most productive solutions for web development, combining simplicity, scalability, and a mature ecosystem. By applying best practices and leveraging its advanced features, developers can create fast, secure, and scalable applications ready for growth.

CHAPTER 16 – FIBER (GO)

Fiber is a web framework for Go (Golang), designed to be fast, lightweight, and efficient. Inspired by Express.js, it offers a simplified API for developing **REST APIs, microservices,** and high-performance applications.

Built on **Fasthttp,** the fastest HTTP library for Go, Fiber can handle a high volume of requests without compromising performance. It is ideal for applications requiring **low latency, high throughput,** and efficient resource execution.

Fiber's structure prioritizes **simplicity and flexibility,** making backend development in Go more accessible for developers familiar with JavaScript-based frameworks like Express.js.

Key Advantages of Fiber

- **Extreme speed:** Based on Fasthttp, Fiber outperforms other HTTP frameworks in terms of performance.
- **Easy learning curve:** Intuitive API, similar to Express.js.
- **Low memory usage:** Ideal for **serverless applications** and **microservices.**
- **Middleware support:** Built-in middleware for **authentication, CORS, caching,** and **compression.**
- **WebSockets support:** Enables real-time bidirectional communication.

Installation and Basic Configuration

Fiber is installed using **Go Modules,** Go's official dependency management tool. First, create a new project:

bash

```bash
mkdir myapi
cd myapi
go mod init myapi
```

Next, install Fiber:

bash

```bash
go get -u github.com/gofiber/fiber/v2
```

After installation, start a basic Fiber server:

go

```go
package main

import (
        "github.com/gofiber/fiber/v2"
)

func main() {
        app := fiber.New()

        app.Get("/", func(c *fiber.Ctx) error {
        return c.SendString("Hello, Fiber!")
        })

        app.Listen(":3000")
}
```

Run the code with:

bash

```bash
go run main.go
```

The server will be available on **port 3000,** ready to receive requests.

Main Features and Differentiators

Fiber stands out due to its **optimized performance** and ease of use. Some of its key features include:

- **Simplified development:** API inspired by Express.js, reducing the learning curve.
- **Built-in middleware:** Native support for **authentication, logging, caching,** and **CORS.**
- **Efficient JSON handling:** Easy serialization and deserialization of data.
- **Optimized routing:** High-performance route handling.
- **WebSockets support:** Enables real-time applications such as **chats, notifications,** and **live dashboards.**
- **Database compatibility:** Native integration with **GORM, MongoDB, PostgreSQL, MySQL,** and **Redis.**
- **Asynchronous execution:** Efficiently handles concurrent request processing.

These features make **Fiber a strategic choice** for modern and scalable backend development.

Use Cases and When to Choose It

Fiber is ideal for applications requiring high performance and low latency. Some of its primary use cases include:

- **REST APIs and microservices:** Backend services optimized for high throughput.
- **Real-time streaming and communication:** WebSocket-based **chat applications, notifications,** and **dashboards.**
- **High-performance data processing:** Applications handling a large number of concurrent requests.
- **API gateways:** Acting as an intermediary between clients and multiple backend services.

- **Serverless backends:** Efficient execution in **AWS Lambda, Google Cloud Functions,** and other cloud environments.

For larger, more structured applications, frameworks such as Gin or Echo may provide better architectural organization.

Practical Demonstration with Code

A **REST API** for task management using Fiber follows a **handler function-based approach** for request handling.

Defining the Data Model

A **Task** model can be created to represent the data:

go

```go
package main

type Task struct {
        ID      int    `json:"id"`
        Title   string `json:"title"`
        Completed bool  `json:"completed"`
}
```

Creating an Array to Store Tasks

A temporary array to hold tasks can be defined as follows:

go

```go
var tasks = []Task{
        {ID: 1, Title: "Learn Fiber", Completed: false},
        {ID: 2, Title: "Create REST API", Completed: false},
}
```

Implementing Controller Functions

The functions to handle tasks are structured as follows:

go

```go
func listTasks(c *fiber.Ctx) error {
        return c.JSON(tasks)
}

func createTask(c *fiber.Ctx) error {
        var newTask Task
        if err := c.BodyParser(&newTask); err != nil {
        return c.Status(400).SendString("Error processing
request")
        }
        newTask.ID = len(tasks) + 1
        tasks = append(tasks, newTask)
        return c.Status(201).JSON(newTask)
}

func updateTask(c *fiber.Ctx) error {
        id := c.Params("id")
        for i, task := range tasks {
        if task.ID == id {
        if err := c.BodyParser(&tasks[i]); err != nil {
        return c.Status(400).SendString("Error processing
request")
        }
        return c.JSON(tasks[i])
        }
        }
        return c.Status(404).SendString("Task not found")
}

func deleteTask(c *fiber.Ctx) error {
        id := c.Params("id")
```

```go
for i, task := range tasks {
if task.ID == id {
tasks = append(tasks[:i], tasks[i+1:]...)
return c.Status(204).SendString("")
}
}
return c.Status(404).SendString("Task not found")
}
```

Defining API Routes

With the handler functions implemented, define the API routes:

go

```go
func main() {
        app := fiber.New()

        app.Get("/tasks", listTasks)
        app.Post("/tasks", createTask)
        app.Put("/tasks/:id", updateTask)
        app.Delete("/tasks/:id", deleteTask)

        app.Listen(":3000")
}
```

This API provides the following endpoints:

- **GET /tasks** – Returns all tasks.
- **POST /tasks** – Creates a new task.
- **PUT /tasks/:id** – Updates an existing task.
- **DELETE /tasks/:id** – Removes a task from the system.

Common Errors and How to Fix Them

Error: "module declares its path as: example.com/

mymodule"

- **Cause:** The project was not properly initialized with go mod init.
- **Solution:** Run:

bash

go mod init myapi

before installing dependencies.

Error: "Port already in use" when starting the server

- **Cause:** Another application is running on port **3000**.
- **Solution:** Change the port to **3001** in app.Listen(":3001").

Error: "EOF while parsing JSON body" when sending a POST request

- **Cause:** The request body was not sent correctly as JSON.
- **Solution:** Ensure the request includes the **Content-Type: application/json** header.

Best Practices and Optimization

To maximize the efficiency of Fiber, consider these best practices:

- **Use middlewares** for **authentication, security,** and **logging.**
- **Configure detailed logs** for monitoring and debugging.
- **Implement caching** to optimize frequently queried data.
- **Enable response compression** to reduce bandwidth usage.

Alternatives and Competing Frameworks

Fiber competes with other high-performance Go frameworks:

- **Gin:** More structured and widely adopted for large-scale

applications.
- **Echo:** Lightweight and optimized for modular applications.
- **Chi:** Designed for building REST APIs with a focus on modularity.

Fiber stands out as one of the best choices for web development in Go, offering high performance, simplicity, and support for modern architectures. By applying best practices and leveraging its advanced features, developers can build robust, secure, and scalable APIs ready for production.

CHAPTER 17 – LARAVEL (PHP)

Laravel is a full-stack framework for web development in PHP, known for its simplicity, elegance, and productivity. Designed to facilitate the construction of **APIs, web applications,** and **robust systems,** it follows the **Model-View-Controller (MVC)** pattern to organize code in a modular and reusable manner.

Unlike minimalist frameworks, Laravel comes with a **complete infrastructure** for authentication, routing, database handling, caching, and security. Its goal is to reduce development complexity, allowing programmers to focus on business logic instead of spending time configuring the environment.

Laravel's philosophy is based on three principles:

- **Simplicity** – Facilitates writing clean and well-structured code.
- **Efficiency** – Seamless integration with databases, queues, and APIs.
- **Security** – Protection against **SQL injection, CSRF,** and common web attacks.

With native support for Eloquent ORM, JWT authentication, asynchronous queues, and event handling, Laravel has become one of the most popular frameworks for building scalable and secure backend applications.

Installation and Basic Configuration

Laravel can be installed using **Composer,** PHP's package manager. First, ensure that **PHP** and **Composer** are installed on your system:

bash

```
composer create-project --prefer-dist laravel/laravel
my_application
cd my_application
php artisan serve
```

The server will start on **port 8000,** allowing you to access the application via **http://127.0.0.1:8000/.**

The Laravel project structure includes:

- **routes/** – Defines application routes.
- **app/Models/** – Database models.
- **app/Http/Controllers/** – Controllers handling requests.
- **database/migrations/** – Database table structure.
- **resources/views/** – Blade template files.

To create a basic controller, run:

bash

```
php artisan make:controller HomeController
```

This generates a **HomeController.php** file where actions can be defined.

Key Features and Differentiators

Laravel provides a **comprehensive set of tools** that simplify backend development:

- **Eloquent ORM:** Object-oriented database handling without writing raw SQL.
- **Flexible routing:** Route definitions and middleware for endpoint protection.
- **Built-in authentication:** Native support for **login, permissions,** and **JWT authentication.**
- **Asynchronous queues:** Background task processing to

optimize performance.

- **Blade template engine:** Separation between logic and application views.
- **Automated testing:** Support for **PHPUnit** and **Laravel Dusk** for end-to-end testing.
- **Easy integration:** Compatibility with **Redis, MySQL, PostgreSQL,** and third-party services.

These features make Laravel one of the most complete frameworks for developing APIs and enterprise applications.

Use Cases and When to Choose It

Laravel is widely used in applications that require structured organization, security, and scalability. Some key scenarios include:

- **RESTful APIs:** Backend services for **front-end** and **mobile** applications.
- **E-commerce and marketplaces:** Order management, payments, and user control.
- **Administrative systems and dashboards:** Enterprise data management.
- **SaaS applications:** Multi-user platforms with complex access rules.
- **Financial systems:** Security and control over online transactions.

For lightweight projects or microframeworks, SlimPHP or Lumen (a lightweight version of Laravel) may be more efficient alternatives.

Practical Demonstration with Code

Creating a REST API for task management in Laravel follows the Model-View-Controller (MVC) pattern.

Creating the Data Model

The first step is to generate a **Task model** with the desired structure:

bash

```
php artisan make:model Task -m
```

This creates the **Task** entity and its database migration in **database/migrations/**. The **Task.php** file can be defined as follows:

php

```
namespace App\Models;

use Illuminate\Database\Eloquent\Factories\HasFactory;
use Illuminate\Database\Eloquent\Model;

class Task extends Model
{
    use HasFactory;

    protected $fillable = ['title', 'completed'];
}
```

Creating a Controller for Task Management

To manage tasks, create a controller with:

bash

```
php artisan make:controller TaskController --resource
```

In the **TaskController.php** file, define methods for handling tasks:

php

```
namespace App\Http\Controllers;
```

```php
use App\Models\Task;
use Illuminate\Http\Request;

class TaskController extends Controller
{
    public function index()
    {
        return response()->json(Task::all());
    }

    public function store(Request $request)
    {
        $task = Task::create($request->all());
        return response()->json($task, 201);
    }

    public function update(Request $request, $id)
    {
        $task = Task::findOrFail($id);
        $task->update($request->all());
        return response()->json($task);
    }

    public function destroy($id)
    {
        Task::destroy($id);
        return response()->json(null, 204);
    }
}
```

Defining API Routes

In the **routes/api.php** file, define the API routes:

php

```
use App\Http\Controllers\TaskController;

Route::apiResource('tasks', TaskController::class);
```

This configuration provides the following endpoints:

- **GET /tasks** – Retrieves all tasks.
- **POST /tasks** – Creates a new task.
- **PUT /tasks/{id}** – Updates a task.
- **DELETE /tasks/{id}** – Deletes a task.

Common Errors and How to Fix Them

Error: "Class 'App\Http\Controllers\Task' not found"

- **Cause:** The model namespace was not imported correctly.
- **Solution:** Add **use App\Models\Task;** at the beginning of the controller.

Error: "SQLSTATE[HY000]: No such table: tasks"

- **Cause:** The database was not migrated correctly.
- **Solution:** Run:

bash

```
php artisan migrate
```

Error: "419 Page Expired" when submitting a form

- **Cause:** CSRF token validation failure.
- **Solution:** Add **@csrf** in Blade forms or disable protection for APIs using **except** in middleware.

Best Practices and Optimization

To keep a **Laravel application efficient** and **scalable,** consider the following practices:

- **Use caching** for performance improvement (**Redis, Memcached**).
- **Avoid excessive data loading** by using **paginate().**
- **Implement secure authentication** with **JWT** or **Laravel Sanctum.**
- **Use Jobs and Queues** for background task processing.
- **Manage permissions** with **Policies and Gates** for granular security.

Alternatives and Competing Frameworks

Laravel competes directly with other popular backend frameworks:

- **Symfony (PHP):** More modular, suitable for enterprise applications.
- **Django (Python):** A full-stack structure similar to Laravel but in Python.
- **Express.js (Node.js):** A minimalist alternative for fast API development.
- **Spring Boot (Java):** Geared towards **enterprise-level applications.**

Laravel stands out as one of the best options for web development and API creation, combining simplicity, scalability, and a complete infrastructure. By applying best practices and leveraging its advanced features, developers can build fast, secure, and production-ready systems.

MODULE 3: FRAMEWORKS FOR APIS AND GRAPHQL – SYSTEM COMMUNICATION

The development of modern APIs has become an essential pillar for application integration, enabling efficient communication between different systems and services. In this module, we explore frameworks specialized in creating RESTful **APIs, GraphQL, and RPC**, analyzing their characteristics, benefits, and differences from traditional approaches.

The frameworks covered in this module were selected based on performance, scalability, and ease of implementation, allowing developers to choose the best solution for their needs. The evolution of APIs goes beyond the traditional REST model, incorporating new technologies such as **GraphQL and RPC (Remote Procedure Call)**, which offer greater flexibility in data request and manipulation.

The first set of frameworks presented includes **Apollo GraphQL, Hasura, and GraphQL Yoga,** which represent the new paradigm of GraphQL-based APIs. These solutions allow clients to make customized queries, retrieving only the necessary data without the rigidity of traditional REST endpoints.

Next, we explore **tRPC and LoopBack**, frameworks that offer hybrid solutions between REST and RPC, facilitating the construction of strongly typed and scalable APIs. These technologies provide greater control over backend-to-frontend operations, promoting efficient integrations and secure data handling.

Additionally, this module includes **FastAPI (Python) and Hapi.js,** two of the most robust frameworks for building high-performance RESTful APIs. While FastAPI stands out for its speed and native support for async/await, Hapi.js offers a modular and secure approach to backend development in JavaScript.

This module provides a comprehensive overview of the most modern technologies for system communication, detailing each framework with practical installation steps, code examples, framework comparisons, and guidelines for performance and security optimization. By the end, you will be equipped to choose the best approach for creating scalable and efficient APIs, aligned with market demands.

CHAPTER 18 – APOLLO GRAPHQL

Apollo GraphQL is a framework for creating and consuming GraphQL APIs, offering a flexible, efficient, and scalable solution for communication between clients and servers. Developed to overcome the limitations of the REST model, Apollo allows applications to request exactly the data they need, optimizing performance and reducing network overhead.

GraphQL, created by Facebook, introduced a new approach to frontend-backend interaction, enabling dynamic queries and structured data returns according to the client's needs. Apollo GraphQL stands out as the most robust implementation of this technology, providing advanced tools for **caching, state management,** and **asynchronous request handling.**

Its main objectives include:

- Improving **data traffic efficiency** by allowing flexible queries.
- Facilitating **data composition and aggregation** from multiple sources.
- Reducing backend complexity by providing a **single endpoint** for all queries.
- Offering a **complete ecosystem** for both **GraphQL clients and servers.**

Apollo GraphQL is widely used in web, mobile, and microservices applications, ensuring efficient communication between multiple services and clients.

Installation and basic configuration

To install Apollo Server and start a GraphQL server, Node.js must be installed. Installation can be done via npm or yarn:

bash

```
npm install @apollo/server graphql
```

Or using Yarn:

bash

```
yarn add @apollo/server graphql
```

After installation, a basic GraphQL server can be started with the following code:

javascript

```
import { ApolloServer } from "@apollo/server";
import { startStandaloneServer } from "@apollo/server/
standalone";

const typeDefs = `
  type Query {
    greeting: String
  }
`;

const resolvers = {
  Query: {
    greeting: () => "Hello, Apollo GraphQL!",
  },
};

const server = new ApolloServer({ typeDefs, resolvers });
```

```
startStandaloneServer(server, { listen: { port:
4000 } }).then(({ url }) => {
  console.log(`Apollo GraphQL server running at ${url}`);
});
```

When running the file, the GraphQL server will start on port 4000, allowing queries in the GraphQL Playground via http:// localhost:4000.

A simple query can be executed directly in the Playground:

graphql

```
query {
  greeting
}
```

The server will respond with:

json

```
{
  "data": {
    "greeting": "Hello, Apollo GraphQL!"
  }
}
```

This initial setup provides an understanding of how Apollo GraphQL processes requests and organizes backend data.

Main features and differentiators

Apollo GraphQL stands out for its **comprehensive feature set**, optimized for efficient and scalable GraphQL API development:

- **Centralized schema:** A single entry point for all API queries.

- **Dynamic queries:** Clients request only the necessary data, reducing network consumption.
- **Subscriptions support:** Real-time communication with WebSockets.
- **Cache persistence:** Integration with Apollo Client to optimize repeated calls.
- **Microservices support:** Composition of distributed GraphQL schemas.
- **Query validation:** Prevention of excessive or unauthorized requests.
- **Monitoring tools:** Apollo Studio and Apollo Gateway for performance analysis.

With these features, Apollo GraphQL becomes a **strategic solution** for companies looking to **optimize APIs** and enhance the **user experience.**

Use cases and when to choose it

Apollo GraphQL is ideal for projects requiring efficient data handling and flexibility in client-server communication. Some of the main use cases include:

- **APIs for modern frontend applications:** Reduces multiple REST calls.
- **Integration between microservices:** Unifies distributed data into a **single endpoint.**
- **Systems requiring dynamic responses:** Such as **interactive dashboards** and **SaaS applications.**
- **Mobile platforms:** Reduces network traffic by consuming only the necessary data.
- **Real-time applications:** Uses subscriptions for **notifications, chat,** and **live updates.**

For systems requiring extremely fast execution and lower complexity, traditional REST APIs or gRPC solutions may be more suitable.

Practical demonstration with code

Building a complete GraphQL API with Apollo can include database handling, authentication, and permissions validation.

Creating a GraphQL schema for tasks

The first step is defining a schema that represents the available operations in the API:

javascript

```
const typeDefs = `
  type Task {
    id: ID!
    title: String!
    completed: Boolean!
  }

  type Query {
    listTasks: [Task]
  }

  type Mutation {
    addTask(title: String!): Task
  }
`;
```

Creating resolvers for data handling

Resolvers execute GraphQL operations:

javascript

```
const tasks = [];

const resolvers = {
```

```
  Query: {
    listTasks: () => tasks,
  },
  Mutation: {
    addTask: (_, { title }) => {
      const newTask = { id: tasks.length + 1, title, completed:
false };
      tasks.push(newTask);
      return newTask;
    },
  },
};
```

Starting the Apollo GraphQL server

javascript

```javascript
const server = new ApolloServer({ typeDefs, resolvers });

startStandaloneServer(server, { listen: { port:
4000 } }).then(({ url }) => {
  console.log(`Apollo GraphQL server running at ${url}`);
});
```

Executing queries and mutations

A query to list all tasks:

graphql

```graphql
query {
  listTasks {
    id
    title
```

```
    completed
  }
}
```

Creating a new task via mutation:

graphql

```
mutation {
  addTask(title: "Learn GraphQL") {
    id
    title
    completed
  }
}
```

These operations demonstrate how Apollo GraphQL **efficiently manages state**, allowing greater flexibility in data consumption.

Common errors and how to fix them

Error: "Cannot query field on type Query"

- **Cause:** The queried field does not exist in the schema.
- **Solution:** Ensure the field is correctly defined in typeDefs.

Error: "Network error: Failed to fetch" in Apollo Client

- **Cause:** The GraphQL server is not accessible.
- **Solution:** Ensure the Apollo Server is running on the correct port.

Error: "Syntax Error: Unexpected Name"

- **Cause:** Incorrect syntax in the GraphQL query.
- **Solution:** Review the query structure to ensure compliance with GraphQL.

Best practices and optimization

To ensure **performance and security** in Apollo GraphQL APIs, the following best practices are recommended:

- **Implement authentication and authorization** to protect sensitive endpoints.
- **Enable caching in Apollo Client** to reduce unnecessary queries.
- **Use pagination** to prevent excessive data returns.
- **Monitor queries with Apollo Studio** to optimize performance.
- **Use database persistence** for greater data reliability.

Apollo GraphQL stands out as one of the best solutions for flexible and scalable APIs, combining performance, modular structure, and seamless integration with various technologies. By applying best practices and leveraging its advanced features, it is possible to build modern and highly efficient systems.

CHAPTER 19 – HASURA

Hasura is a high-performance GraphQL engine designed to provide an **instant API layer** over PostgreSQL, MySQL, and SQL Server databases. It enables the **automatic creation of GraphQL endpoints** without requiring manual coding, accelerating the development of secure, scalable, and real-time APIs.

Unlike other GraphQL frameworks that require manual schema and resolver definitions, Hasura automatically generates queries, mutations, and subscriptions based on the database structure. This significantly reduces development time, making it an ideal solution for modern applications, microservices, and serverless architectures.

Its main objectives include:

- Automating the creation of **GraphQL APIs** without manually writing resolvers.
- Providing an **efficient authentication** and **access control** mechanism.
- Facilitating **integration with external data sources**, such as **REST APIs** and third-party services.
- **Enabling real-time queries** via subscriptions for interactive applications.

Hasura is widely adopted in SaaS applications, analytical dashboards, and platforms that require rapid database integration.

Installation and basic configuration

Hasura can run **locally, in Docker containers,** or **in cloud services.** The fastest way to start a Hasura server is via Docker:

bash

```
docker run -d -p 8080:8080 \
  -e HASURA_GRAPHQL_DATABASE_URL=postgres://
user:password@host:5432/database_name \
  -e HASURA_GRAPHQL_ENABLE_CONSOLE=true \
  hasura/graphql-engine:v2.14.0
```

This command:

- Starts a **Hasura server** on port **8080**.
- Connects to a **PostgreSQL database**.
- Enables the **Hasura Console** (administrative interface).

Once the container is running, the Hasura Console will be available at:

text

```
http://localhost:8080
```

With the web interface, it is possible to view, modify, and query the database directly via GraphQL, without manually configuring endpoints.

Main features and differentiators

Hasura stands out for its ability to instantly transform relational databases into optimized GraphQL APIs. Among its main features are:

- **Automatic GraphQL API generation:** The API is dynamically created based on the database structure.
- **Optimized mutations and queries:** Operations are automatically constructed, eliminating the need for manual resolvers.
- **Real-time subscriptions:** Native support for automatic notifications via **WebSockets.**

- **Granular access control:** Detailed **permissions per user** and **dynamic access rules.**
- **Efficient query execution:** Integration with **caching** and **performance optimization** mechanisms.
- **Compatibility with REST APIs:** Allows **GraphQL and REST** to be combined in the same endpoint.
- **Support for microservices: Efficient communication** between distributed services.

With these capabilities, Hasura positions itself as one of the fastest and most scalable solutions for GraphQL backend development.

Use cases and when to choose it

Hasura is recommended for projects that require **efficient GraphQL APIs** without manually developing resolvers. Some key scenarios include:

- **SaaS applications:** Rapid development of **multi-user** APIs.
- **Data analytics platforms: Dynamic dashboards** and reports.
- **Real-time APIs: Monitoring applications** and **live notifications.**
- **Integration with microservices: Efficient communication** between databases and REST services.
- **Serverless backends:** Execution of **GraphQL queries** in **scalable environments.**

For applications requiring full API customization, frameworks like Apollo Server may offer greater flexibility.

Practical demonstration with code

The Hasura API can be tested directly in the Hasura Console, which automatically generates GraphQL endpoints based on database tables.

Creating a database model

After connecting Hasura to **PostgreSQL,** a **tasks table** can be created via the Console:

sql

```sql
CREATE TABLE tasks (
  id SERIAL PRIMARY KEY,
  title TEXT NOT NULL,
  completed BOOLEAN DEFAULT FALSE
);
```

This table will automatically be converted into GraphQL queries and mutations.

Querying data with GraphQL

Hasura's API allows retrieving **all tasks** with the following query:

graphql

```graphql
query {
  tasks {
    id
    title
    completed
  }
}
```

Creating a new task via mutation

graphql

```graphql
mutation {
  insert_tasks(objects: { title: "Learn Hasura", completed:
false }) {
```

```
    returning {
      id
      title
      completed
    }
  }
}
```

Updating an existing task

graphql

```
mutation {
  update_tasks(where: { id: { _eq: 1 } }, _set: { completed: true }) {
    returning {
      id
      title
      completed
    }
  }
}
```

Deleting a task

graphql

```
mutation {
  delete_tasks(where: { id: { _eq: 1 } }) {
    returning {
      id
    }
  }
}
```

Activating Subscriptions for real-time notifications

graphql

```
subscription {
  tasks {
    id
    title
    completed
  }
}
```

With this setup, any database changes will be automatically reflected for all connected clients.

Common errors and how to fix them

Error: "Failed to connect to database"

- **Cause:** Incorrect PostgreSQL configuration.
- **Solution:** Check if the **connection string** in HASURA_GRAPHQL_DATABASE_URL is correct.

Error: "Permission denied for table tasks"

- **Cause: Incorrect permissions configuration** in the Hasura Console.
- **Solution:** Define **access rules** in the **permissions settings.**

Error: "subscription field not found" when executing a Subscription

- **Cause:** The database **does not support real-time events.**
- **Solution: Enable subscriptions** and **WebSockets** support in Hasura.

Best practices and optimization

To ensure **high performance** and **security** in the Hasura API, some best practices should be adopted:

- **Enable caching** to reduce database load.
- **Restrict access permissions** to protect sensitive data.
- **Use WebSockets** for **real-time updates only when necessary.**
- **Monitor logs** and **optimize GraphQL queries** using **Apollo Studio** or other analysis tools.
- **Enable support for Actions and Remote Schemas** to extend functionality **beyond the database.**

Alternatives and competing frameworks

Hasura competes directly with other GraphQL and traditional REST API solutions:

- **Apollo GraphQL:** Offers **greater flexibility** and **custom resolver** implementation.
- **Prisma + GraphQL Yoga:** An alternative for **manual GraphQL** integration.
- **Django Graphene:** A solution for **Python projects** requiring **GraphQL.**
- **Express + REST APIs:** For applications that **still prefer a REST model.**

Hasura stands out as one of the fastest and most efficient options for GraphQL backend development, enabling the creation of robust and scalable APIs without complexity. With automatic endpoint generation, granular access control, and subscription support, it solidifies itself as one of the most productive solutions for modern microservices development.

CHAPTER 20 – GRAPHQL YOGA

GraphQL Yoga is a **lightweight and highly optimized framework** for building GraphQL servers in **Node.js** and **TypeScript**. Designed for **simplicity, efficiency,** and **compatibility** with any environment, it stands out as **one of the easiest solutions** to quickly set up a **GraphQL API.**

Unlike other implementations, GraphQL Yoga is designed to work without complex configuration, providing a ready-to-use experience. It is based on GraphQL.js (the official GraphQL library), ensuring high compatibility with the GraphQL ecosystem and allowing integrations with Express.js, Fastify, and even Serverless Functions.

Its main objectives include:

- Providing an **optimized GraphQL API** without complexity
- Ensuring **compatibility** with any web framework
- Offering **native support for subscriptions**
- Facilitating the creation of **scalable and high-performance GraphQL servers**

GraphQL Yoga is widely used in microservices, modern frontend applications, and systems requiring a simplified GraphQL setup.

Installation and basic configuration

GraphQL Yoga can be installed directly in **Node.js** or **TypeScript** projects using npm or yarn:

bash

```
npm install graphql-yoga graphql
```

Or with yarn:

bash

```
yarn add graphql-yoga graphql
```

After installation, a **basic GraphQL server** can be started with:

javascript

```javascript
import { createServer } from "graphql-yoga";

const typeDefs = `
  type Query {
    greeting: String
  }
`;

const resolvers = {
  Query: {
    greeting: () => "Hello, GraphQL Yoga!",
  },
};

const server = createServer({ schema: { typeDefs, resolvers } });

server.start(() => {
  console.log("GraphQL Yoga server running on port 4000");
});
```

The **GraphQL Yoga server** will be started on **port 4000,** ready to receive requests via **GraphQL Playground** at:

text

http://localhost:4000

A **simple query** can be executed to test the server:

graphql

```
query {
  greeting
}
```

The returned response will be:

json

```
{
  "data": {
    "greeting": "Hello, GraphQL Yoga!"
  }
}
```

This initial setup helps understand how GraphQL Yoga processes GraphQL requests and delivers optimized responses.

Key features and differentiators

GraphQL Yoga stands out for performance, flexibility, and scalability. Its key features include:

- **Native support for subscriptions** via **WebSockets for real-time communication**
- **Compatibility with any Node.js framework**, including **Express.js, Fastify,** and **Serverless**
- **Optimized performance** with **asynchronous execution** and **efficient query handling**
- **Middleware support** for **authentication and authorization** control

- **Seamless integration** with **databases and external services**
- **Zero initial configuration,** enabling a **GraphQL API** with just a few lines of code

These features make GraphQL Yoga one of the simplest and most powerful options for building GraphQL APIs.

Use cases and when to choose it

GraphQL Yoga is ideal for projects that need flexible, easy-to-configure GraphQL APIs. Some key use cases include:

- **Backend APIs** for modern frontend applications using **React, Vue.js,** or **Angular**
- **Microservices** and **backend integrations** for **distributed architectures**
- **Real-time systems** requiring **subscriptions** via **WebSockets**
- **Serverless APIs** for cloud platforms like **AWS Lambda** and **Google Cloud Functions**
- **Prototypes and rapid application development**, where **minimal configuration** is essential

For applications requiring greater control over resolvers and internal logic, frameworks like Apollo Server may be more suitable.

Practical demonstration with code

Building a complete GraphQL API with GraphQL Yoga involves defining a schema, resolvers, and integrating with dynamic data.

Creating a GraphQL schema for tasks

The first step is defining a **GraphQL schema** that represents the data structure:

javascript

```
const typeDefs = `
```

```
type Task {
  id: ID!
  title: String!
  completed: Boolean!
}

type Query {
  listTasks: [Task]
}

type Mutation {
  addTask(title: String!): Task
}

type Subscription {
  newTask: Task
}
`;
```

Creating resolvers for handling data

Resolvers handle **GraphQL operations** and return requested data:

javascript

```javascript
const tasks = [];
const { PubSub } = require("graphql-yoga");

const pubsub = new PubSub();

const resolvers = {
  Query: {
    listTasks: () => tasks,
  },
```

```
  Mutation: {
    addTask: (_, { title }) => {
      const newTask = { id: tasks.length + 1, title, completed:
false };
      tasks.push(newTask);
      pubsub.publish("NEW_TASK", { newTask });
      return newTask;
    },
  },
  Subscription: {
    newTask: {
      subscribe: () => pubsub.asyncIterator("NEW_TASK"),
    },
  },
};
```

Starting the GraphQL Yoga server

javascript

```
const server = createServer({ schema: { typeDefs, resolvers } });

server.start(() => {
  console.log("GraphQL Yoga server running on port 4000");
});
```

Executing queries and mutations

A query to list all tasks:

graphql

```
query {
  listTasks {
    id
```

```
    title
    completed
  }
}
```

Creating a **new task** via **mutation**:

graphql

```
mutation {
  addTask(title: "Learn GraphQL Yoga") {
    id
    title
    completed
  }
}
```

Activating a subscription to receive **real-time updates**:

graphql

```
subscription {
  newTask {
    id
    title
    completed
  }
}
```

With this setup, any new task added will be automatically sent to all connected clients.

Common errors and how to resolve them

Error: "Cannot query field on type Query"

- **Cause:** The queried field is **not defined** in typeDefs.
- **Solution:** Verify that the field is **correctly declared and spelled.**

Error: "Network error: Failed to fetch" in GraphQL client

- **Cause:** The **GraphQL server** is **not accessible.**
- **Solution:** Ensure the **Yoga server** is running on the **correct port.**

Error: "Subscription field not found" when using subscriptions

- **Cause: WebSockets** are **not enabled.**
- **Solution:** Properly configure **PubSub** and enable **WebSockets** support on the server.

Best practices and optimization

To maintain an **efficient and secure** GraphQL Yoga server, follow these **best practices:**

- **Implement authentication and authorization** to **restrict access** to sensitive queries
- **Use pagination** to **avoid excessive data returns** in queries
- **Monitor request logs** to identify **bottlenecks** and optimize queries
- **Enable response compression** to **improve API performance**
- **Use caching** to **reduce server load** and **accelerate responses**

Alternatives and competing frameworks

GraphQL Yoga competes with various GraphQL implementations, including:

- **Apollo Server:** Provides **greater control** over resolvers and API state
- **Hasura:** An **instant GraphQL API** over relational

databases
- **Express + GraphQL.js:** A manual setup for **greater customization**

GraphQL Yoga is one of the simplest, most efficient, and scalable options for building GraphQL servers, offering optimized performance and easy integration with any modern web technology.

CHAPTER 21 – TRPC

tRPC is a **framework for secure communication** between frontend and backend, designed to **eliminate the need for manually writing API-consuming code.** It enables **strongly typed remote procedure calls (RPC),** ensuring that TypeScript types are shared between the backend and frontend **without requiring code generation or additional schemas.**

Unlike GraphQL or REST, which require manually defining endpoints and data structures, tRPC infers types directly from the server code, ensuring that the client always knows what data it can request, with complete type safety at compile time.

Its main objectives include:

- **Eliminating boilerplate code** in client-server communication.
- **Providing compile-time type safety** to prevent API call errors.
- **Ensuring a seamless developer experience** for TypeScript projects.
- **Facilitating scalable applications** without requiring a traditional GraphQL or REST server.

tRPC is widely adopted in full-stack TypeScript applications, such as Next.js, React, and Node.js, ensuring a smooth development experience.

Installation and basic setup

tRPC can be installed and configured **easily** in a **Node.js + TypeScript** environment. To get started, install the required packages:

bash

```
npm install @trpc/server @trpc/client @trpc/react @trpc/
next zod
```

The package @trpc/server is used on the **backend**, while @trpc/client and @trpc/react provide **frontend integration.** Zod is used for **validation and type definition**, ensuring **data security** in API calls.

Creating a tRPC server

A **basic server** can be set up using **Express.js** and **tRPC** as follows:

typescript

```typescript
import express from "express";
import { initTRPC } from "@trpc/server";
import { z } from "zod";

const t = initTRPC.create();

// Router definition
const appRouter = t.router({
  greeting: t.procedure
    .input(z.string().optional())
    .query((({ input }) => `Hello, ${input || "world"}!`),
});

export type AppRouter = typeof appRouter;

const app = express();

app.use("/trpc", (req, res) => {
  return appRouter.createCaller({}).greeting("User");
});
```

```
app.listen(4000, () => {
  console.log("tRPC server running on port 4000");
});
```

With this setup, a tRPC server runs on port 4000, ready to receive frontend requests without manually defining REST or GraphQL endpoints.

Key features and differentiators

tRPC stands out for its innovative approach to backend-frontend communication, removing the complexity of API creation. Its key features include:

- **Automatic type inference** with no need for **manual JSON or GraphQL schemas.**
- **Zero boilerplate**, eliminating **the need to create REST controllers or GraphQL resolvers.**
- **Built-in input and output validation** with **Zod support.**
- **Support for asynchronous calls and WebSockets** for **real-time communication.**
- **Compatibility with Next.js, React, Vue.js, and other frontend frameworks.**
- **Scalability** for **complex applications** without requiring a **GraphQL backend.**

These features make tRPC one of the most efficient solutions for client-server communication in modern TypeScript projects.

Use cases and when to choose it

tRPC is ideal for full-stack TypeScript projects, enabling seamless integration between frontend and backend. Some key use cases include:

- **Next.js applications:** Native **tRPC integration** without requiring an external API.

- **Internal APIs for microservices:** Secure communication between different system components.
- **Developer experience-focused applications: Faster development** with **reduced maintenance effort.**
- **Systems requiring strong type safety: Automatic validation** of API calls.
- **An alternative to GraphQL** for **TypeScript applications** with **less complexity** and **no need for a dedicated GraphQL server.**

For applications that require compatibility with multiple languages, solutions like GraphQL, gRPC, or REST may be more suitable.

Practical demonstration with code

Building a complete system using tRPC + React involves defining backend procedures and consuming data in the frontend.

Creating a tRPC router for task management

typescript

```
const tasksRouter = t.router({
  list: t.procedure.query(() => [
    { id: 1, title: "Learn tRPC", completed: false },
    { id: 2, title: "Build a secure API", completed: true },
  ]),

  add: t.procedure
    .input(z.object({ title: z.string() }))
    .mutation(({ input }) => ({
      id: Math.random(),
      title: input.title,
      completed: false,
    })),
```

```
});
```

Consuming the API in the frontend with React

typescript

```typescript
import { trpc } from "../utils/trpc";

const TaskList = () => {
  const { data, isLoading } = trpc.tasks.list.useQuery();

  if (isLoading) return <p>Loading...</p>;

  return (
    <ul>
      {data?.map((task) => (
        <li key={task.id}>{task.title}</li>
      ))}
    </ul>
  );
};
```

Adding a new task from the frontend

typescript

```typescript
const AddTask = () => {
  const mutation = trpc.tasks.add.useMutation();

  const add = () => {
    mutation.mutate({ title: "New task" });
  };

  return <button onClick={add}>Add Task</button>;
};
```

With this setup, the application **consumes and modifies** backend data using **TypeScript type safety.**

Common errors and how to resolve them

Error: "Cannot query field on type Query"

- **Cause:** The queried field is **not defined** in the **tRPC router.**
- **Solution:** Ensure the method is **properly registered** on the backend.

Error: "Failed to fetch" in the frontend

- **Cause:** The **tRPC backend** is **not running.**
- **Solution:** Ensure the server is **started on the correct port.**

Error: "Invalid input" when calling a mutation

- **Cause:** The sent data does **not match** the z.object() schema.
- **Solution:** Verify that the **data structure** follows the **expected model.**

Best practices and optimization

To ensure high performance and security when using tRPC, follow these best practices:

- **Use Zod** for **data validation** to avoid unexpected errors.
- **Configure permissions** to **restrict access** to sensitive procedures.
- **Enable caching** to **optimize frequent queries.**
- **Integrate WebSockets** for **real-time notifications.**
- **Monitor API call logs** to identify **performance bottlenecks.**

Alternatives and competing frameworks

tRPC differs from other traditional solutions for backend/ frontend communication:

- **GraphQL (Apollo, Yoga):** Requires **manual resolver and schema definitions,** while **tRPC automatically infers types.**
- **Traditional REST APIs:** Require **manual route and controller definitions,** while **tRPC reduces complexity.**
- **gRPC:** Provides **high-performance multi-language support** but is **more complex** than **tRPC** for **TypeScript applications.**

With strong type safety, simplified development, and zero boilerplate, tRPC emerges as the best solution for efficient client-server communication in full-stack TypeScript applications.

CHAPTER 22 – LOOPBACK

LoopBack is a **framework for scalable API development in Node.js,** designed to simplify the creation of **backend applications** with **easy integration** into databases, authentication, and automatic generation of **RESTful and GraphQL APIs.** Initially developed by **StrongLoop** and now maintained by the **OpenJS Foundation**, LoopBack is widely used in **enterprise systems** due to its **modular architecture, support for microservices,** and **flexibility in connecting to various data sources.**

Unlike minimalist frameworks like Express.js, LoopBack provides a complete environment for backend development, allowing automatic endpoint creation based on data models. Its primary goal is to reduce development time by providing an architecture that eliminates repetitive API code.

Key Benefits

- **Automatic data modeling** based on **TypeScript or JSON schemas.**
- **Dynamic API creation** without manually defining **REST endpoints.**
- **Native GraphQL support** for **flexible queries.**
- **Built-in user management and authentication.**
- **Compatibility with SQL, NoSQL, and other data sources.**

LoopBack is widely adopted by companies looking for a robust framework for microservices, enterprise APIs, and scalable backend applications.

Installation and Basic Configuration

LoopBack can be installed globally via **npm** to facilitate **project creation:**

bash

```
npm install -g @loopback/cli
```

After installation, a new project can be initialized with:

bash

```
lb4 app my-api
cd my-api
npm start
```

The lb4 app command initializes a complete project, including basic configuration, directory structure, and TypeScript support.

The generated structure includes:

- src/models/ – Definition of **data models.**
- src/repositories/ – **Database access management.**
- src/controllers/ – **Business logic and API endpoints.**
- src/datasources/ – **Database connection setup.**

With the **server running,** API endpoints can be accessed via **Swagger UI** at:

bash

```
http://localhost:3000/explorer
```

Key Features and Differentiators

LoopBack stands out for its modular and scalable approach to backend development, offering features that reduce API complexity.

- **Automatic RESTful API creation** based on **data models.**
- **Native GraphQL support** without additional configuration.
- **Built-in authentication and access control** with **JWT and OAuth.**
- **Connectors for SQL and NoSQL databases** (MySQL, PostgreSQL, MongoDB, Redis).
- **Integration with external services** such as **REST APIs, SOAP, and gRPC.**
- **User and role-based permission management.**
- **Extensibility with middlewares and microservices.**

These features make LoopBack one of the most complete options for backend development, providing a productive environment for rapid API creation.

Use Cases and When to Choose It

LoopBack is ideal for projects that require **rapid development** of **scalable APIs** and **connections to multiple data sources.**

Primary use cases include:

- **Enterprise systems** that need **modular APIs** for service integration.
- **SaaS platforms** supporting **multiple databases and secure authentication.**
- **Microservices development** for **distributed architectures.**
- **Applications requiring advanced user control and permissions.**
- **Backend APIs** for **mobile and web applications.**

If the goal is to build a minimalistic API without advanced features, frameworks like Express.js or Fastify may be more suitable.

Practical Demonstration with Code

Creating a Data Model in LoopBack

A **task model** can be created quickly using the **CLI:**

bash

lb4 model

When prompted, provide the following details:

- **Model name:** Task
- **Attributes:**
  - id: number (Primary Key)
  - title: string
  - completed: boolean

This will generate a file in src/models/task.model.ts:

typescript

```typescript
import {Entity, model, property} from '@loopback/repository';

@model()
export class Task extends Entity {
  @property({
    type: 'number',
    id: true,
    generated: true,
  })
  id: number;

  @property({
    type: 'string',
    required: true,
  })
  title: string;

  @property({
```

```
  type: 'boolean',
  default: false,
})
completed: boolean;
}
```

Creating a Repository for Database Access

To create a **repository** for handling **database operations,** run:

bash

```
lb4 repository
```

Select TaskRepository and link it to a **database source.** This will generate a file in src/repositories/task.repository.ts:

typescript

```
import {DefaultCrudRepository} from '@loopback/repository';
import {Task} from '../models';
import {inject} from '@loopback/core';
import {DbDataSource} from '../datasources';

export class TaskRepository extends DefaultCrudRepository<
  Task,
  typeof Task.prototype.id
> {
  constructor(@inject('datasources.db') dataSource:
DbDataSource) {
    super(Task, dataSource);
  }
}
```

Creating a Controller to Expose the REST API

Finally, the **API can be generated automatically** with:

bash

```
lb4 controller
```

Selecting **TaskController** will create a controller to expose **REST endpoints:**

typescript

```
import {repository} from '@loopback/repository';
import {TaskRepository} from '../repositories';
import {post, get, requestBody} from '@loopback/rest';
import {Task} from '../models';

export class TaskController {
  constructor(
    @repository(TaskRepository)
    public taskRepo: TaskRepository,
  ) {}

  @post('/tasks')
  async create(@requestBody() task: Task) {
    return this.taskRepo.create(task);
  }

  @get('/tasks')
  async list() {
    return this.taskRepo.find();
  }
}
```

With the **server running,** the following **endpoints will be**

available:

- POST /tasks – Create a new task
- GET /tasks – List all tasks

This allows the creation of **RESTful APIs** without **manual endpoint definition.**

Common Errors and How to Fix Them

Error: "Datasource not found"

- **Cause:** The **database** was **not configured correctly.**
- **Solution:** Properly configure the file **datasources/db.datasource.ts.**

Error: "Validation failed" when trying to create a record

- **Cause:** The **object sent does not match** the **expected model.**
- **Solution:** Ensure that the **submitted attributes** match those defined in **task.model.ts.**

Error: "Access denied" when accessing an endpoint

- **Cause: Access permissions** were **not configured.**
- **Solution:** Define **authentication rules** for each route in **TaskController.ts.**

Best Practices and Optimization

To ensure **performance and security**, some **best practices** should be followed:

- **Use caching** to optimize **frequent queries.**
- **Implement JWT authentication** to protect **sensitive endpoints.**
- **Monitor logs and performance metrics** using **LoopBack Observer.**
- **Utilize middlewares** for **data validation** and **permission control.**

Alternatives and Competing Frameworks

LoopBack competes directly with frameworks such as:

- **NestJS** – More flexible but requires **manual configuration** of models and endpoints.
- **FastAPI (Python)** – Alternative for **high-performance** and **rapid development.**
- **Express.js** – A **simpler** framework without **built-in authentication or data models.**

LoopBack stands out as one of the most complete solutions for backend development, eliminating repetitive code and enabling rapid creation of robust APIs.

CHAPTER 23 – FASTAPI (PYTHON)

FastAPI is a **high-performance web framework** for developing **RESTful and GraphQL APIs with Python**. Designed to offer **speed, security, and ease of use**, FastAPI stands out for its **native integration with Pydantic** and support for **Python Type Hints**, enabling **automatic data validation** and **interactive documentation generation** without requiring manual configuration.

Built to be as fast as asynchronous frameworks like Node.js and Go, FastAPI leverages Python's async/await execution to provide a more efficient API. Its primary goal is to reduce complexity in backend development, offering a productive and highly optimized environment for building scalable services.

Key Advantages

- **Extremely fast execution** (almost as fast as **Node.js** and **Go**).
- **Automatic data validation** using **Pydantic** and **Type Hints**.
- **Automatically generated interactive documentation** with **OpenAPI** and **Swagger UI**.
- **Native support** for **WebSockets, Background Tasks, and GraphQL**.
- **Compatibility with SQL and NoSQL databases**, including **PostgreSQL, MySQL, and MongoDB**.

FastAPI is widely used in microservices, machine learning applications, process automation, and high-performance APIs.

Installation and Basic Configuration

To install **FastAPI** and an **ASGI server** (such as **Uvicorn**), use the following command:

bash

```
pip install fastapi uvicorn
```

After installation, a **FastAPI server** can be started quickly with the following code:

python

```
from fastapi import FastAPI

app = FastAPI()

@app.get("/")
async def root():
    return {"message": "FastAPI API is active"}

if __name__ == "__main__":
    import uvicorn
    uvicorn.run(app, host="0.0.0.0", port=8000)
```

The server will be available at:

bash

```
http://127.0.0.1:8000
```

To access the **automatically generated interactive documentation**, visit:

bash

http://127.0.0.1:8000/docs

Key Features and Differentiators

FastAPI is designed to maximize API development efficiency, providing a set of features that differentiate it from other frameworks:

- **Native asynchronous execution**, optimizing the performance of applications handling multiple concurrent requests.
- **Automatic data validation** using **Type Hints** and **Pydantic**.
- **Automatic interactive documentation** generation with **OpenAPI and Swagger UI**.
- **Simplified database integration** with **PostgreSQL, MySQL, and MongoDB**.
- **Native support for WebSockets and GraphQL**, enabling real-time communication.
- **Robust authentication and authorization**, making it easier to implement **API security**.

These features make FastAPI one of the most modern and efficient options for developing REST and GraphQL APIs in Python.

Use Cases and When to Choose It

FastAPI is ideal for projects requiring high performance, data validation, and automatic documentation.

Some of the **primary use cases** include:

- **Microservices and distributed systems** that need **fast and scalable APIs**.
- **APIs for machine learning and artificial intelligence**, optimized for **production-ready models**.
- **SaaS platforms**, where **security and input validation** are

fundamental.
- **Process automation** and **system integration**.
- **High-load systems**, such as **data streaming APIs** and **interactive dashboards**.

If the goal is to build minimal APIs without automatic validation or integrated documentation, frameworks like Flask may be more suitable.

Practical Demonstration with Code

Defining the Data Model with Pydantic

python

```python
from pydantic import BaseModel

class Item(BaseModel):
    id: int
    name: str
    price: float
```

Creating RESTful Endpoints

python

```python
from fastapi import FastAPI
from typing import List

app = FastAPI()

# Temporary database
database = []

@app.post("/items/", response_model=Item)
async def create_item(item: Item):
    database.append(item)
    return item
```

```
@app.get("/items/", response_model=List[Item])
async def list_items():
    return database

@app.get("/items/{item_id}", response_model=Item)
async def get_item(item_id: int):
    for item in database:
        if item.id == item_id:
            return item
    return {"error": "Item not found"}

@app.delete("/items/{item_id}")
async def delete_item(item_id: int):
    global database
    database = [item for item in database if item.id != item_id]
    return {"message": "Item successfully removed"}
```

By executing this code, the API will be ready for CRUD operations, with automatic data validation and interactive documentation support.

Common Errors and How to Fix Them

Error: "ModuleNotFoundError: No module named 'fastapi'"

- **Cause: FastAPI** is not installed.
- **Solution:** Install it using **pip install fastapi uvicorn.**

Error: "TypeError: object NoneType is not subscriptable"

- **Cause:** Trying to access a **nonexistent index**.
- **Solution:** Ensure that the **requested ID** exists in the list before accessing it.

Error: "Cannot import name 'BaseModel' from 'pydantic'"

- **Cause: Incompatible Pydantic version.**

- **Solution: Update** to the latest version using pip install -U pydantic.

Best Practices and Optimization

To ensure high performance and security when using FastAPI, some recommended practices include:

- **Using asynchronous database connections** to avoid **I/O bottlenecks.**
- **Configuring CORS correctly** to ensure **secure external access.**
- **Implementing JWT authentication** to **protect sensitive endpoints.**
- **Monitoring logs and performance metrics** to **optimize the API.**
- **Enabling caching** to **reduce server load** on **frequent queries.**

Alternatives and Competing Frameworks

FastAPI stands out from other **popular Python API frameworks:**

- **Flask – Simple and flexible,** but lacks **native validation** and **asynchronous execution.**
- **Django REST Framework – Robust and integrated with Django,** but **heavier.**
- **Tornado – Focused on high-concurrency asynchronous applications,** but lacks **OpenAPI integration.**

The combination of speed, automatic validation, and interactive documentation makes FastAPI one of the best options for building modern, high-performance APIs in Python.

CHAPTER 24 – HAPI.JS

Hapi.js is a **web framework for Node.js** designed to provide **security, scalability, and flexibility** in the development of APIs and backend applications. Created as an alternative to **Express.js**, Hapi.js stands out for its **modular architecture, robust data validation system,** and **native plugin support**, allowing developers to build **secure and scalable APIs** without requiring additional libraries.

Its focus is on security and detailed request control, making it widely used in enterprise systems, RESTful APIs, and applications requiring advanced authentication and permission management.

Key Benefits

- **Declarative and modular configuration** for easier management of routes and plugins.
- **Automatic data validation** using the **Joi** library.
- **Native support for authentication and authorization**, including **JWT, OAuth,** and **API Keys**.
- **Advanced request management capabilities**, such as **rate limiting**.
- **Flexibility in creating microservices** and **scalable applications**.

Hapi.js is widely used in enterprise APIs, payment systems, SaaS platforms, and high-traffic applications.

Installation and Basic Configuration

Hapi.js can be installed directly via **npm** or **yarn**:

bash

```bash
npm install @hapi/hapi
```

Or, using **yarn**:

bash

```bash
yarn add @hapi/hapi
```

After installation, a **basic server** can be configured with just a few lines of code:

javascript

```javascript
const Hapi = require('@hapi/hapi');

const startServer = async () => {
  const server = Hapi.server({
    port: 3000,
    host: 'localhost'
  });

  server.route({
    method: 'GET',
    path: '/',
    handler: () => ({ message: 'Hapi.js API is active' })
  });

  await server.start();
  console.log('Server running at:', server.info.uri);
};

startServer();
```

Running this code, the **Hapi.js server** will start on **port 3000** and can be accessed at:

bash

http://localhost:3000

The **declarative configuration** of **Hapi.js** allows for intuitive **route and middleware** management, providing **better organization** in backend application development.

Key Features and Differentiators

Hapi.js is designed to offer security, extensibility, and easy maintenance in backend applications. Among its key features are:

- **Simplified route management**, allowing a **modular and reusable** structure.
- **Automatic input data validation** using the **Joi** library.
- **Integrated authentication and authorization**, eliminating the need for **external libraries**.
- **Native plugin support**, enabling framework extension **without impacting performance**.
- **Middleware for request control**, such as **rate limiting** and **CORS**.
- **WebSocket support**, allowing **bidirectional real-time communication**.

These features make Hapi.js one of the most secure and flexible solutions for building scalable APIs in Node.js.

Use Cases and When to Choose

Hapi.js is recommended for projects requiring advanced security, modularity, and detailed request control. Its main use cases include:

- **Financial and payment systems**, where **security** and **data validation** are essential.
- **APIs for enterprise applications**, requiring **robust**

authentication and **granular access control.**

- **SaaS platforms**, needing **scalable and extensible APIs.**
- **Microservices**, where **modularity** and **plugin support** facilitate **maintenance.**
- **Data streaming applications**, with **WebSockets** and **asynchronous event support.**

If the goal is to develop simple and lightweight APIs, without advanced request control, frameworks like Express.js may be a more straightforward alternative.

Practical Demonstration with Code

Defining the Data Model and Validation

javascript

```javascript
const Joi = require('@hapi/joi');

const taskSchema = Joi.object({
  id: Joi.number().integer().required(),
  title: Joi.string().min(3).required(),
  completed: Joi.boolean().default(false)
});
```

Creating a Temporary Database and CRUD Endpoints

javascript

```javascript
const Hapi = require('@hapi/hapi');
const Joi = require('@hapi/joi');

const database = [];

const startServer = async () => {
  const server = Hapi.server({
    port: 3000,
    host: 'localhost'
```

```
  });

  server.route([
    {
      method: 'POST',
      path: '/tasks',
      handler: (request, h) => {
        const { error, value } =
taskSchema.validate(request.payload);
        if (error) return h.response({ error:
error.details[0].message }).code(400);

        database.push(value);
        return h.response(value).code(201);
      }
    },
    {
      method: 'GET',
      path: '/tasks',
      handler: () => database
    },
    {
      method: 'GET',
      path: '/tasks/{id}',
      handler: (request, h) => {
        const task = database.find(t => t.id ==
request.params.id);
        if (!task) return h.response({ error: "Task not
found" }).code(404);
        return task;
      }
    },
```

```
{
  method: 'DELETE',
  path: '/tasks/{id}',
  handler: (request, h) => {
    const index = database.findIndex(t => t.id ==
request.params.id);
    if (index === -1) return h.response({ error: "Task not
found" }).code(404);

    database.splice(index, 1);
    return h.response({ message: "Task successfully
removed" }).code(200);
  }
}
]);

await server.start();
console.log('Server running at:', server.info.uri);
};

startServer();
```

This code allows creating, listing, and deleting tasks in a temporary database, using automatic validation with Joi to ensure data integrity.

Common Errors and How to Fix Them

Error: "Cannot find module '@hapi/hapi'"

- **Cause:** Hapi.js **is not installed correctly**.
- **Solution:** Reinstall with **npm install @hapi/hapi**.

Error: "Payload validation failed" when sending a **POST request**

- **Cause:** The **sent data does not match the defined**

schema.

- **Solution:** Check that the **required fields** are correct.

Error: "Route not found" when accessing a URL

- **Cause:** The **endpoint was not defined correctly.**
- **Solution:** Confirm the **route structure** in the code.

Best Practices and Optimization

To ensure efficiency and security when using Hapi.js, some recommended practices include:

- **Using authentication middleware** to **protect sensitive routes.**
- **Configuring CORS correctly** to **prevent unauthorized access.**
- **Enabling detailed logs** to **monitor errors and performance.**
- **Using caching in frequent requests** to **reduce server load.**
- **Setting request limits (rate limiting)** to **prevent DDoS attacks.**

Alternatives and Competing Frameworks

Hapi.js differs from other popular backend development solutions in Node.js:

- **Express.js – Simple and flexible**, but lacks **native authentication and plugin support.**
- **Fastify – Faster**, but with **fewer integrated features** than **Hapi.js.**
- **NestJS – TypeScript-based**, focused on **scalable and modular architectures.**

The combination of security, robust validation, and plugin support makes Hapi.js one of the best choices for developing secure and scalable APIs.

MODULE 4: FULL-STACK FRAMEWORKS – COMPLETE DEVELOPMENT

Full-stack development requires **integrated solutions** that unify **frontend and backend** efficiently, simplifying implementation and improving productivity. Frameworks designed for this purpose **reduce code complexity**, ensuring **structural consistency, security, scalability**, and **high performance**. This module explores some of the **best available options**, providing an overview of their **features and applications**.

The adoption of **full-stack frameworks** is a strategic choice for developers who want a **cohesive development environment**, eliminating the need to configure multiple technologies separately. These frameworks offer **benefits** such as **efficient state management, built-in APIs, native authentication support**, and **database integration**, allowing complete applications to be built with **less effort and redundant code**. Choosing the right tool can **accelerate product delivery**, making development **faster and more efficient**.

Among the options explored, **RedwoodJS** stands out for its **React- and GraphQL-based architecture**, making it a **robust choice** for **scalable applications** requiring a **well-defined structure**. For developers who prefer a more **familiar and productive** environment, **Blitz.js** emerges as an **option inspired by Ruby on Rails**, providing a **simplified experience** for building **full-stack React applications**.

The module also covers AdonisJS, a framework strongly

influenced by Laravel, bringing a structured approach with advanced backend and frontend features to the Node.js ecosystem. For those looking for reactivity and interactivity, Meteor stands out as a full-stack JavaScript solution that seamlessly integrates frontend and backend, enabling real-time updates and a highly dynamic development process.

Content management is a crucial factor in many modern applications, and Strapi emerges as a flexible headless CMS, enabling efficient API management and seamless integration with various frontends. Finally, Remix concludes the module with an optimized approach to page loading, ensuring a better user experience by prioritizing rendering efficiency and data flow optimization.

Each framework discussed in this module offers a unique approach, catering to different development needs and scenarios. Throughout the chapters, topics such as installation, configuration, key features, best practices, and problem-solving are covered, allowing developers to deeply understand their applications and determine when to adopt them in their projects.

With this knowledge, professionals will be able to make **strategic decisions** when selecting the **best full-stack technology** for each **requirement**, ensuring **more efficient, scalable,** and **well-structured applications**.

CHAPTER 25 – REDWOODJS

RedwoodJS is a modern full-stack framework for web application development, designed to seamlessly integrate frontend and backend. Based on React, GraphQL, and Prisma, RedwoodJS simplifies the creation of scalable applications without the need to manually configure communication between system layers.

Its primary purpose is to enable developers to build **complex web applications** with the **simplicity of a full-stack framework**, eliminating the need to configure REST APIs or manually manage requests. RedwoodJS follows the **"enhanced JAMstack"** concept, combining **dynamic rendering** and **serverless architecture** to deliver **high performance** and **scalability**.

Some of the key benefits of RedwoodJS include:

- **Native integration** between frontend and backend using GraphQL.
- **Automatic state management** for the entire application.
- **Unified database model** with Prisma ORM.
- **Hybrid rendering** (SSG and SSR) to optimize loading speed.
- **Built-in authentication system**, allowing easy user setup.
- **TypeScript adoption by default**, ensuring development security.

The framework is ideal for startups, MVPs, SaaS platforms, and modern web applications, where development speed and scalability are essential.

Installation and Basic Configuration

To install RedwoodJS, Node.js and Yarn must be installed. The first step is to create a new project:

bash

```
yarn create redwood-app my-application
cd my-application
yarn redwood dev
```

This command initializes a RedwoodJS application with a predefined structure, including frontend, backend, and a GraphQL API.

The generated project structure is organized as follows:

- **api/** – Contains the backend, services, and database configurations.
- **web/** – Frontend directory, based on React and Apollo Client.
- **graphql/** – Definitions of GraphQL queries and mutations.
- **prisma/** – Database configuration and migrations.

Running yarn redwood dev starts both the **frontend and backend**, enabling simultaneous development without manual configuration.

Key Features and Differentiators

RedwoodJS stands out from other full-stack frameworks by **automating communication between frontend and backend**, eliminating the complexity of manually configuring APIs and databases. Its main features include:

- **Embedded GraphQL**, efficiently connecting frontend and backend.
- **Database management with Prisma ORM**, simplifying

data persistence.

- **Automatic code generation**, allowing quick CRUD creation.
- **Built-in authentication and access control**, facilitating user and permission implementation.
- **Integration with serverless services**, enabling scalability and reduced operational costs.

This approach ensures faster development and greater productivity, making RedwoodJS an excellent choice for modern web applications.

Use Cases and When to Choose It

RedwoodJS is ideal for projects that require fast full-stack development without compromising scalability and code organization. Some of its primary use cases include:

- **Startups and MVPs**, where reduced development time is crucial.
- **SaaS platforms**, requiring efficient frontend-backend integration.
- **Modern web applications**, with GraphQL and TypeScript requirements.
- **Serverless systems**, where efficient cloud execution is a key advantage.

If a project requires more control over the backend or integration with specific services not supported by RedwoodJS, frameworks like Next.js or NestJS might be more suitable alternatives.

Practical Demonstration with Code

Defining a Data Model with Prisma

To define a **Task** model, edit the prisma/schema.prisma file:

prisma

model Task {

```
id     Int    @id @default(autoincrement())
title  String
completed Boolean @default(false)
}
```

After defining the model, run the migration to create the database table:

bash

```
yarn rw prisma migrate dev --name create_tasks_table
```

Creating the GraphQL Backend

To automatically generate the CRUD with RedwoodJS, use the following command:

bash

```
yarn rw g scaffold task
```

This automatically creates the **GraphQL service** and **frontend pages**.

Consuming the API on the Frontend

On the frontend, RedwoodJS allows intuitive backend GraphQL consumption. To list tasks, simply create a React component:

javascript

```
import { useQuery, gql } from '@redwoodjs/web'

const LIST_TASKS = gql`
  query {
    tasks {
```

```
      id
      title
      completed
    }
  }
  `

const TaskList = () => {
  const { data, loading } = useQuery(LIST_TASKS)

  if (loading) return <p>Loading...</p>

  return (
    <ul>
      {data.tasks.map(task => (
        <li key={task.id}>{task.title}</li>
      ))}
    </ul>
  )
}

export default TaskList
```

This code fetches and displays the tasks stored in the database using GraphQL and Apollo Client.

Common Errors and How to Fix Them

Error: "GraphQL API is not responding"

- **Cause:** The backend is not running correctly.
- **Solution:** Ensure that yarn redwood dev is active.

Error: "Database does not exist"

- **Cause:** The database was not initialized.
- **Solution:** Run yarn rw prisma migrate dev to create it.

Error: "React Hook useQuery is not defined"

- **Cause:** Missing Apollo Client import.
- **Solution:** Add import { useQuery, gql } from '@redwoodjs/web'.

Best Practices and Optimization

To ensure **efficiency and scalability**, some **best practices** should be followed:

- Use **native authentication** to protect sensitive endpoints.
- Enable **Apollo Client caching** to reduce GraphQL query load.
- Implement **middlewares** for security and input validation.
- Configure **environment variables** to store sensitive credentials.
- Monitor **logs and metrics** to identify performance bottlenecks.

Alternatives and Competing Frameworks

RedwoodJS competes with various modern full-stack frameworks, including:

- **Next.js** – Excellent for **SSR and SSG** applications but lacks built-in GraphQL.
- **Blitz.js** – Inspired by **Ruby on Rails**, but focused exclusively on React.
- **AdonisJS** – A robust alternative for developers who prefer a **structured backend**.

The combination of GraphQL, Prisma, and integrated full-stack architecture makes RedwoodJS one of the most efficient solutions for modern web development, ensuring productivity and scalability for applications of any size.

CHAPTER 26 – BLITZ.JS

Blitz.js is a full-stack framework for web development based on Next.js, designed to provide an integrated and productive development experience. Inspired by Ruby on Rails, Blitz.js eliminates the need to manually configure REST or GraphQL APIs, allowing developers to write full-stack code in a unified manner.

Its key differentiator is the **"Zero API"** system, which enables direct calls from the frontend to the backend without requiring explicit endpoint configurations. Additionally, Blitz.js includes **native authentication support, database management with Prisma,** and **automatic code generation,** making it ideal for startups, MVPs, and SaaS applications.

Some of the main advantages of Blitz.js include:

- **Full-stack architecture** integrated with Next.js.
- **"Zero API" system**, eliminating the need to manually configure APIs.
- **Native support for Prisma ORM**, simplifying data persistence.
- **Built-in authentication and permission management.**
- **Automatic CRUD code generation.**

With this approach, Blitz.js allows developers to build modern web applications faster and more efficiently without sacrificing flexibility.

Installation and Basic Configuration

To install Blitz.js, Node.js and Yarn must be set up. The first step to starting a new project is to run:

bash

```
npm install -g blitz
blitz new my-application
cd my-application
blitz dev
```

This command creates a **pre-configured Blitz.js application**, including both frontend and backend.

The generated project structure includes:

- **app/** – Contains frontend components and backend functions.
- **db/** – Database configuration and Prisma ORM settings.
- **pages/** – Next.js files for routing.
- **integrations/** – Authentication and external service configurations.

Running blitz dev starts the development server and allows local application access.

Key Features and Differentiators

Blitz.js stands out for its **integrated full-stack development approach**, eliminating the need for manual API configuration. Its main features include:

- **"Zero API" system**, allowing direct communication between frontend and backend.
- **Built-in authentication system**, supporting **JWT and OAuth**.
- **Automatic code generation**, enabling **fast CRUD creation**.
- **Native support for Prisma ORM**, simplifying **database access**.
- **Full compatibility with Next.js**, supporting **SSR and SSG**.

With these features, Blitz.js provides one of the most productive experiences for full-stack development with JavaScript and TypeScript.

Use Cases and When to Choose It

Blitz.js is ideal for developers who need to build full-stack applications quickly, without worrying about manual API setup. Some of the primary use cases include:

- **Startups and MVPs**, where reduced development time is crucial.
- **SaaS applications**, requiring integrated authentication and data persistence.
- **Platforms with intensive CRUD operations**, benefiting from **automatic code generation**.
- **Next.js-based systems**, where **SSR and SSG integration** is an advantage.

If a project requires more control over the API or follows a more traditional approach, frameworks like Next.js (standalone) or NestJS may be more suitable alternatives.

Practical Demonstration with Code

Defining the Data Model with Prisma

In the db/schema.prisma file, the **Task** model can be defined as follows:

prisma

```prisma
model Task {
  id    Int   @id @default(autoincrement())
  title String
  completed Boolean @default(false)
}
```

After configuring the model, update the database with:

bash

```
blitz prisma migrate dev --name create_tasks_table
```

Automatically Generating CRUD Operations

Blitz.js allows generating a **complete set of CRUD operations** for a model automatically:

bash

```
blitz generate all task
```

This command creates:

- **React pages and components** for task display.
- **Backend functions** for **creating, listing, editing, and deleting tasks**.
- **Automatic Prisma integration** for database access.

Creating an Endpoint to List Tasks

Inside app/tasks/queries/getTasks.ts, define the function to fetch all tasks:

typescript

```
import db from "db"

export default async function getTasks() {
  return await db.task.findMany()
}
```

Consuming the Backend in the Frontend

To display the tasks in the frontend, Blitz.js uses the useQuery hook:

typescript

```
import { useQuery } from "blitz"
import getTasks from "app/tasks/queries/getTasks"

const TaskList = () => {
  const [tasks] = useQuery(getTasks, null)

  return (
    <ul>
      {tasks.map((task) => (
        <li key={task.id}>{task.title}</li>
      ))}
    </ul>
  )
}

export default TaskList
```

The task list will **automatically be displayed**, without the need to configure **REST or GraphQL requests**.

Common Errors and How to Fix Them

Error: "Prisma Client is not defined"

- **Cause:** Prisma was not initialized correctly.
- **Solution:** Run blitz prisma generate to regenerate the Prisma client.

Error: "Cannot find module 'blitz'"

- **Cause:** Project dependencies were not installed.
- **Solution:** Run yarn install or npm install to install dependencies.

Error: "Hook useQuery is not a function"

- **Cause:** Incorrect Blitz.js import.
- **Solution:** Ensure useQuery is correctly imported from

blitz.

Best Practices and Optimization

To ensure security and efficiency when using Blitz.js, some best practices are recommended:

- **Set up authentication correctly** to **protect restricted pages**.
- **Use React Query caching** to optimize backend queries.
- **Manage user permissions** to restrict actions within the system.
- **Monitor logs and performance metrics** to identify bottlenecks.
- **Use environment variables** to store sensitive credentials.

Alternatives and Competing Frameworks

Blitz.js competes with various modern full-stack frameworks, including:

- **Next.js** – Excellent for **SSR and SSG**, but lacks **"Zero API"**.
- **RedwoodJS** – An alternative based on **GraphQL**, focused on **scalable applications**.
- **AdonisJS** – A structured **Node.js alternative**, resembling **Laravel**.

The "Zero API" approach of Blitz.js eliminates complexity in full-stack development, making it one of the most productive options for building modern web applications.

CHAPTER 27 – ADONISJS

AdonisJS is a full-stack framework for Node.js, inspired by Laravel, designed to provide a robust, productive, and secure structure for web applications and API development. Unlike minimalist frameworks like Express.js, AdonisJS takes a more structured approach, allowing developers to work with ORM, authentication, data validation, and other integrated features without the need for external libraries.

The primary goal of AdonisJS is to offer a **consistent and efficient development environment**, where developers can focus on business logic without excessive configuration. It is ideal for those looking for a **powerful backend framework** that is well-organized and has a **fluid syntax** based on JavaScript and TypeScript.

Some of the main advantages of AdonisJS include:

- **Organized code structure** based on conventions.
- **Integrated ORM (Lucid)** for SQL database management.
- **Ready-to-use authentication and user management**.
- **Built-in data validation system**.
- **WebSockets support** for real-time communication.
- **Modular and expandable framework** with plugin support.

This approach makes AdonisJS an excellent choice for developers who want a structured and complete framework for **building scalable APIs and web applications**.

Installation and Basic Configuration

To install AdonisJS, Node.js and npm must be set up. A new project can be created using the following command:

bash

```
npm init adonis-ts-app@latest my-application
cd my-application
node ace serve --watch
```

The command node ace serve --watch starts the development server, allowing changes to be applied automatically.

The default structure of AdonisJS includes the following directories:

- **app/** – Contains the main backend files, including models and controllers.
- **config/** – Global application settings.
- **database/** – Migration scripts and database connection files.
- **resources/** – Templates and public files.
- **start/** – Initial framework configuration.

The default application already includes a **router, basic authentication, and ORM support**, ensuring that developers can get started quickly.

Key Features and Differentiators

AdonisJS stands out as a **full-stack framework** that combines power and simplicity, offering features that eliminate the need for external packages for common functionalities. Some of the key differentiators include:

- **Lucid ORM** for seamless SQL database integration.
- **Built-in authentication and permissions management**.
- **Flexible middleware system** for security and logging.
- **Robust data validation system** with dynamic schema support.
- **WebSockets support** for real-time applications.
- **Modular structure**, allowing efficient code organization.

These features make AdonisJS one of the most complete backend frameworks for Node.js, ensuring productivity and security.

Use Cases and When to Choose It

AdonisJS is ideal for projects that require organization, security, and efficiency in backend development. Some of its primary use cases include:

- **RESTful and GraphQL APIs**, which require a structured and secure backend.
- **Authentication and user management systems**, due to its **native support for JWT and OAuth**.
- **SaaS applications and web platforms**, where modularity and scalability are essential.
- **Financial and banking systems**, which demand **strict validation and advanced security**.
- **Real-time communication platforms**, utilizing **WebSockets and asynchronous events**.

If the project requires a more minimalist approach, frameworks like Express.js or Fastify may be more suitable.

Practical Demonstration with Code

Creating a Data Model with Lucid ORM

The first step to working with a database in AdonisJS is to create a model using Lucid ORM. To generate a Task model, use the following command:

bash

```
node ace make:model Task
```

In the file **app/Models/Task.ts**, define the model as follows:

typescript

```
import { BaseModel, column } from '@ioc:Adonis/Lucid/Orm'

export default class Task extends BaseModel {
  @column({ isPrimary: true })
  public id: number

  @column()
  public title: string

  @column()
  public completed: boolean
}
```

After defining the model, create the **migration file** for the database:

bash

```
node ace make:migration create_tasks_table
```

Edit the generated file in **database/migrations/** to define the table structure:

typescript

```
import BaseSchema from '@ioc:Adonis/Lucid/Schema'

export default class Tasks extends BaseSchema {
  protected tableName = 'tasks'

  public async up() {
    this.schema.createTable(this.tableName, (table) => {
      table.increments('id')
      table.string('title').notNullable()
      table.boolean('completed').defaultTo(false)
```

```
    table.timestamps(true)
  })
}

public async down() {
  this.schema.dropTable(this.tableName)
}
}
```

Run the migration to create the table:

bash

```bash
node ace migration:run
```

Creating Routes and Controllers

Generate a controller to handle **task operations**:

bash

```bash
node ace make:controller Task
```

In the file **app/Controllers/Http/TaskController.ts**, define the CRUD methods:

typescript

```typescript
import Task from 'App/Models/Task'

export default class TaskController {
  public async list() {
    return await Task.all()
  }

  public async create({ request }) {
```

```
  const data = request.only(['title', 'completed'])
  return await Task.create(data)
 }

 public async delete({ params }) {
   const task = await Task.findOrFail(params.id)
   await task.delete()
   return { message: 'Task successfully removed' }
 }
}
```

Defining Routes in start/routes.ts

typescript

```
import Route from '@ioc:Adonis/Core/Route'
import TaskController from 'App/Controllers/Http/
TaskController'

Route.get('/tasks', 'TaskController.list')
Route.post('/tasks', 'TaskController.create')
Route.delete('/tasks/:id', 'TaskController.delete')
```

Now, the API is functional, allowing task creation, listing, and deletion.

Common Errors and How to Fix Them

Error: "Cannot find module '@ioc:Adonis/Lucid/Orm'"

- **Cause:** Lucid ORM is not installed correctly.
- **Solution:** Run npm install @adonisjs/lucid and node ace migration:run.

Error: "Database connection refused"

- **Cause:** Incorrect database configuration.
- **Solution:** Edit the **.env** file and verify the access

credentials.

Error: "Route not found" when accessing the API

- **Cause:** The route is incorrectly configured or not registered.
- **Solution:** Ensure the correct structure in **start/routes.ts**.

Best Practices and Optimization

To ensure efficiency and security when using AdonisJS, some best practices are recommended:

- **Use authentication middleware** to **protect restricted routes**.
- **Enable detailed logging** for **monitoring and debugging**.
- **Manage user permissions** to restrict **sensitive actions**.
- **Use caching** to optimize **database queries**.

Alternatives and Competing Frameworks

AdonisJS is comparable to several modern backend frameworks:

- **Express.js** – More minimalist but lacks built-in ORM and authentication.
- **NestJS** – Based on TypeScript and more modular but has a **steeper learning curve**.
- **Fastify** – Focused on performance but lacks an **integrated structure**.

The combination of simplicity, organization, and built-in features makes AdonisJS one of the best options for backend development in Node.js, ensuring productivity and scalability.

CHAPTER 28 – METEOR

Meteor is a full-stack JavaScript framework designed to provide an integrated and highly productive development experience. It enables developers to build complete web and mobile applications using a single language across the entire stack. Meteor simplifies development by integrating frontend, backend, and database into a single environment, reducing the need to configure multiple separate technologies.

With native support for reactivity and real-time communication, Meteor is one of the best choices for **dynamic applications, interactive dashboards, and systems requiring instant data updates**. It uses **Node.js** on the backend and easily integrates with popular libraries such as **React, Vue.js, and Angular**.

Some of the **main benefits** of Meteor include:

- **Unified code for frontend and backend**, eliminating discrepancies between the two sides of the application.
- **Native support for reactivity and real-time updates**, reducing the need for manual polling.
- **Integrated MongoDB database** and simplified abstraction with MiniMongo.
- **Automated dependency and update management**, avoiding configuration issues.
- **Compatibility with modern frontend libraries**, such as React and Vue.js.
- **Simplified deployment** with support for cloud environments and continuous integration.

These features make Meteor an excellent choice for highly interactive and real-time collaborative applications.

Installation and Basic Configuration

Meteor can be installed directly via the command line, allowing quick project creation. To install Meteor, use:

bash

```
curl https://install.meteor.com/ | sh
```

After installation, a new project can be created with:

bash

```
meteor create my-application
cd my-application
meteor npm install
meteor run
```

This command initializes a complete development environment, including the server, database, and integrated frontend. Meteor runs on port 3000 by default and can be accessed locally at:

arduino

```
http://localhost:3000
```

The structure of a **Meteor project** includes:
- **/client** – Frontend files and UI components.
- **/server** – Backend logic and database connection.
- **/imports** – Modules shared between frontend and backend.
- **/public** – Static files, such as images and fonts.

This organization ensures a clear separation of responsibilities and facilitates maintenance.

Key Features and Differentiators

Meteor stands out for offering a unified full-stack environment, eliminating the need to manually configure different technologies. Some of its main features include:

- **MongoDB database** with automatic synchronization between client and server.
- **MiniMongo**, a local database for offline operations and reactivity.
- **Native support for WebSockets and DDP (Distributed Data Protocol)** for instant communication.
- **Hot code push**, enabling code updates **without requiring a reinstall** on mobile devices.
- **Native integration with modern frontend libraries**, such as **React and Vue.js**.
- **Integrated build and deployment tools**, allowing **quick publication** to cloud servers.

These features make Meteor one of the most efficient options for creating interactive and collaborative applications.

Use Cases and When to Choose It

Meteor is recommended for projects requiring high interactivity, real-time reactivity, and fast development. Some use cases include:

- **Collaborative applications**, such as **chats, task management tools, and interactive dashboards**.
- **Monitoring and notification systems**, which require **instant data updates**.
- **E-learning and online education platforms**, supporting **virtual classrooms and real-time interactions**.
- **SaaS applications**, where **fast deployment and scalability** are essential.
- **MVPs and rapid prototyping**, reducing development time.

If a project requires more granular backend control or demands greater database flexibility, frameworks such as Next.js or NestJS may be more suitable alternatives.

Practical Demonstration with Code

Creating a Task Collection in the Database

Meteor uses MongoDB as its default database. To define a task collection, create the file /imports/api/tasks.js:

javascript

```javascript
import { Mongo } from 'meteor/mongo'

export const Tasks = new Mongo.Collection('tasks')
```

Defining Methods in the Backend

In the **/server/main.js** file, import the collection and create methods to manipulate data:

javascript

```javascript
import { Meteor } from 'meteor/meteor'
import { Tasks } from '../imports/api/tasks'

Meteor.startup(() => {
  if (Tasks.find().count() === 0) {
    Tasks.insert({ title: 'First task', completed: false })
  }
})

Meteor.methods({
  'tasks.insert'(title) {
    Tasks.insert({ title, completed: false })
  },
```

```
'tasks.remove'(id) {
  Tasks.remove(id)
},
'tasks.toggle'(id, status) {
  Tasks.update(id, { $set: { completed: status } })
}
})
```

Creating the Frontend with React

To display tasks on the frontend, create a React component in **/client/Tasks.jsx**:

javascript

```
import React from 'react'
import { useTracker } from 'meteor/react-meteor-data'
import { Tasks } from '../imports/api/tasks'

const TaskList = () => {
  const tasks = useTracker(() => Tasks.find().fetch())

  const addTask = () => {
    const title = prompt('Enter the task title:')
    Meteor.call('tasks.insert', title)
  }

  return (
    <div>
      <button onClick={addTask}>New Task</button>
      <ul>
        {tasks.map((task) => (
          <li key={task._id}>
            {task.title}
```

```
        <button onClick={() => Meteor.call('tasks.remove',
task._id)}>Remove</button>
      </li>
    ))}
  </ul>
</div>
)
}
```

export default TaskList

This code allows listing, adding, and removing tasks with real-time communication.

Common Errors and How to Fix Them

Error: "Mongo is not defined"

- **Cause:** MongoDB import was not done correctly.
- **Solution:** Ensure that import { Mongo } from 'meteor/mongo' is present in the code.

Error: "Method not found" when calling a method

- **Cause:** The method was not correctly registered on the server.
- **Solution:** Confirm that the methods are **defined in / server/main.js**.

Error: "Cannot find module 'meteor/meteor'"

- **Cause:** Meteor dependencies were not installed correctly.
- **Solution:** Run meteor npm install to ensure all required libraries are available.

Best Practices and Optimization

To ensure **better performance and security** when using Meteor, consider the following best practices:

- **Use asynchronous methods** to optimize **database operations**.
- **Protect method calls** with security rules to prevent **unauthorized access**.
- **Enable logs and monitoring**, ensuring quick issue detection.
- **Enable frontend caching**, reducing unnecessary calls to the server.
- **Use environment variables** to store sensitive credentials securely.

Alternatives and Competing Frameworks

Meteor competes with various modern full-stack frameworks, such as:

- **Next.js** – Excellent for **SSR and SSG**, but lacks **native MongoDB and real-time reactivity**.
- **Blitz.js** – Alternative based on **Next.js**, with support for ORM and a unified architecture.
- **NestJS** – A **more structured backend framework**, but **without native reactivity support**.

With its integrated full-stack approach and native reactivity support, Meteor stands out as one of the best options for developing dynamic and real-time applications.

CHAPTER 29 – STRAPI

Strapi is an open-source framework for API management, designed to provide flexibility, security, and customization in backend application development. It enables developers to quickly create **REST and GraphQL APIs** without the need to configure a backend from scratch.

Strapi's key differentiator is its **headless architecture**, allowing the backend to be decoupled from the frontend, making it possible to integrate with **React, Vue.js, Angular, Flutter, mobile applications, and any other frontend technology**.

The purpose of Strapi is to enable the rapid and efficient development of scalable APIs, eliminating the need to manually program endpoints and providing a graphical interface for content management.

Some of the **main advantages** of Strapi include:

- **Custom API creation without code** via an intuitive interface.
- **Native support for REST and GraphQL**, ensuring flexibility in frontend communication.
- **Built-in authentication and permissions**, simplifying access control.
- **Integrated database management**, supporting **SQL and NoSQL**.
- **Modular system with plugin support**, allowing extensibility and customization.

These features make Strapi one of the best options for developers looking for speed and flexibility in building custom backends.

Installation and Basic Configuration

Installing Strapi is simple and can be done using **Node.js** and **npm**. To create a new project, run:

bash

```
npx create-strapi-app@latest my-application --quickstart
```

This command creates a **Strapi project** and automatically starts the **development server**. The application can be accessed at:

bash

```
http://localhost:1337/admin
```

Upon accessing this URL, the user will be prompted to create an administrator account, allowing configuration of data models, permissions, and content directly through the web panel.

The generated project structure includes:

- **/api** – Directory where **data models and controllers** are located.
- **/config** – Strapi configuration files.
- **/database** – Database configuration, supporting **SQLite, PostgreSQL, or MongoDB**.
- **/public** – Static files accessible externally.
- **/src** – Application source code.

This structure ensures organization and modularity, facilitating maintenance and scalability.

Key Features and Differentiators

Strapi stands out by automating API creation and providing

a complete environment for content and data management. Some of its key features include:

- **Admin panel** to manage APIs and content without coding.
- **Automatic generation of REST and GraphQL endpoints**.
- **Native authentication and access control**, ensuring data security.
- **Support for multiple databases**, including PostgreSQL, MySQL, and SQLite.
- **Extensibility through plugins and custom middleware**.
- **Built-in file upload and media management**.

With these features, **Strapi enables fast and scalable backend creation**, making it ideal for **startups, enterprise applications, and headless platforms**.

Use Cases and When to Choose It

Strapi is recommended for projects that require a robust and flexible backend, without the need to manually code APIs. Some use cases include:

- **APIs for headless websites and blogs**, allowing integration with multiple frontends.
- **SaaS platforms**, where **centralized and secure** data management is required.
- **Enterprise applications**, which demand **detailed authentication and permission control**.
- **E-commerce platforms**, where product and order management is API-driven.
- **Dashboards and administrative systems**, facilitating access to **structured data and reports**.

If the project requires a fully customized backend, with specific business logic and complete architectural control, frameworks like NestJS or AdonisJS may be more suitable.

Practical Demonstration with Code

Creating a Task API in Strapi

Within the admin panel, go to Content-Type Builder and create a new model named Task with the following fields:

- **title (String)** – Stores the task title.
- **description (Text)** – Provides detailed task information.
- **status (Boolean)** – Indicates whether the task is completed.

Once the model is saved, Strapi automatically generates the corresponding REST and GraphQL endpoints.

Consuming the REST API

To **fetch all tasks** via API, make a **GET request** to:

bash

```
curl http://localhost:1337/api/tasks
```

The response will be a **JSON** object containing all stored tasks.

Creating a New Task via API

To **create a new task**, use a **POST request**:

bash

```
curl -X POST http://localhost:1337/api/tasks \
  -H "Content-Type: application/json" \
  -d '{
    "data": {
      "title": "New Task",
      "description": "Task description",
      "status": false
    }
  }'
```

Enabling Public API Access

By default, Strapi restricts API access to authenticated users. To allow public access, go to Settings → Roles & Permissions and enable read permissions for the Public role.

With this configuration, **any frontend application** can **consume API data**.

Common Errors and How to Fix Them

Error: "403 Forbidden" when accessing the API

- **Cause:** Incorrect permission settings.
- **Solution:** Enable permissions in the **admin panel** under **Roles & Permissions**.

Error: "Database connection failed"

- **Cause:** Database not properly configured.
- **Solution:** Edit the file **config/database.js** and ensure credentials are correct.

Error: "Module not found: strapi"

- **Cause:** Strapi dependencies not installed correctly.
- **Solution:** Run npm install to ensure all required libraries are available.

Best Practices and Optimization

To ensure security and efficiency when using Strapi, consider the following best practices:

- **Use SQL databases** such as **PostgreSQL or MySQL** for greater reliability.
- **Properly configure CORS** to avoid blocked external requests.
- **Enable logging and monitoring** to quickly detect API failures.
- **Use JWT or OAuth authentication** to restrict access to

sensitive data.

- **Configure environment variables** to store **database credentials securely**.

Alternatives and Competing Frameworks

Strapi competes with various API management solutions, including:

- **NestJS** – A **modular backend framework based on TypeScript**, ideal for **more customized architectures**.
- **Ghost** – A **headless alternative focused on blogs and content publishing**.
- **Hasura** – A **GraphQL platform** that allows **automatic connection to databases**.

The combination of flexibility, automation, and user-friendly interface makes Strapi one of the best options for creating scalable APIs and backends, ensuring high productivity and seamless frontend integration.

CHAPTER 30 – REMIX

Remix is a full-stack framework for web development, designed to offer better performance, accessibility, and user experience through a **server-side rendering (SSR) and Progressive Enhancement** architecture. Created by the founders of React Router, Remix enables developers to build **fast and responsive applications** by optimizing **loading, navigation, and state management**.

Remix adopts a server-first model, where interactions are processed on the backend before reaching the client. This improves load time, reduces JavaScript usage on the frontend, and maintains a smooth experience even on slow connections.

Some of the **key benefits** of Remix include:

- **Hybrid rendering with SSR and streaming support**.
- **Optimized data management**, eliminating the need for external global state libraries.
- **Progressive loading support**, improving mobile device experience.
- **Direct integration with React Router**, making navigation **dynamic and efficient**.
- **Native support for forms and server-side action handling**.

Remix is ideal for interactive and high-performance web applications, such as e-commerce platforms, dashboards, and applications that require fast loading and fluid navigation.

Installation and Basic Configuration

Remix can be installed using **npm, pnpm, or yarn**. To create a new project, run:

bash

```
npx create-remix@latest my-application
cd my-application
npm install
npm run dev
```

This command generates a **structured project** for **frontend and backend**. The development server runs on **port 3000** and can be accessed at:

bash

```
http://localhost:3000
```

The **Remix project structure** includes:

- **app/** – Contains application files such as components and routes.
- **routes/** – Defines pages and their interactions.
- **entry.server.tsx** – Server entry point.
- **entry.client.tsx** – Client entry point.
- **remix.config.js** – Global configuration file.

This structure facilitates maintenance, modularity, and scalability in web development.

Key Features and Differentiators

Remix stands out by offering an efficient approach to rendering and data loading, reducing the need for extra client-side requests. Some of its key features include:

- **Server-side data loading**, reducing unnecessary client fetch requests.
- **Direct form handling and backend actions**, eliminating the need for additional JavaScript.
- **Server-to-client streaming responses**, ensuring

progressive rendering.

- **Intelligent prefetching**, allowing **route preloading** for better user experience.
- **Enhanced security** by avoiding excessive **frontend data exposure**.

With these features, Remix reduces browser overhead, making it a powerful option for applications that require speed, interactivity, and efficiency.

Use Cases and When to Choose It

Remix is recommended for projects that prioritize performance, user experience, and accessibility. Some of its key use cases include:

- **E-commerce platforms**, where **load speed directly impacts conversions**.
- **SaaS platforms**, requiring **dynamic loading and efficient navigation**.
- **Enterprise applications**, leveraging **SSR for optimized processing**.
- **Blogs and content-based sites**, where **SEO and fast loading** are essential.
- **Interactive dashboards**, demanding **efficient data loading**.

If a project requires more control over APIs and backend logic, frameworks like Next.js or NestJS may be better alternatives.

Practical Demonstration with Code

Creating a Route and Loading Data from the Server

In Remix, **routes** are defined in the **routes/** directory. To create a **tasks page**, create a new file **routes/tasks.tsx**:

tsx

```tsx
import { json, LoaderFunction } from "@remix-run/node"
import { useLoaderData } from "@remix-run/react"
```

```
export const loader: LoaderFunction = async () => {
  const tasks = [
    { id: 1, title: "Learn Remix", completed: false },
    { id: 2, title: "Create an API", completed: true }
  ]
  return json(tasks)
}

export default function Tasks() {
  const tasks = useLoaderData()

  return (
    <div>
      <h1>Task List</h1>
      <ul>
        {tasks.map((task) => (
          <li key={task.id}>
            {task.title} - {task.completed ? "□" : "□"}
          </li>
        ))}
      </ul>
    </div>
  )
}
```

This code creates a /tasks route that loads data directly from the server before rendering, ensuring efficient loading.

Creating an Interactive Form

Remix allows sending data **directly to the backend** without requiring additional client-side state management libraries. To create a **form**, edit **routes/tasks.tsx** and add:

tsx

```
import { Form } from "@remix-run/react"

export function action({ request }) {
  const formData = await request.formData()
  const title = formData.get("title")
  return json({ title, status: "Task added" })
}

export default function Tasks() {
  return (
    <div>
      <h1>Add Task</h1>
      <Form method="post">
        <input type="text" name="title" placeholder="Enter a task" required />
        <button type="submit">Add</button>
      </Form>
    </div>
  )
}
```

With this server-side form handling, Remix eliminates frontend state management overhead, improving efficiency.

Common Errors and How to Fix Them

Error: "useLoaderData is not a function"

- **Cause:** The hook was not imported correctly.
- **Solution:** Ensure the correct import:

tsx

```
import { useLoaderData } from "@remix-run/react"
```

Error: "LoaderFunction must return a JSON response"

- **Cause:** The loader function is not returning a **JSON object**.
- **Solution:** Ensure the function uses return json(data).

Error: "Form submission failed"

- **Cause:** The action function is **not properly defined**.
- **Solution:** Check if the **action function** is correctly **exported and set to POST**.

Best Practices and Optimization

To ensure better performance and security when using Remix, consider:

- **Leveraging SSR and streaming** for faster page load times.
- **Minimizing client-side JavaScript**, taking advantage of server-side data loading.
- **Configuring caching** to improve API response time.
- **Enhancing form security**, preventing data injection attacks.
- **Monitoring logs and performance** to identify bottlenecks.

Alternatives and Competing Frameworks

Remix competes with various **full-stack development frameworks**, such as:

- **Next.js** – A popular **SSR and SSG** alternative, focusing on APIs and React integration.
- **SvelteKit** – A framework based on **Svelte**, offering **efficient and simplified SSR**.
- **Gatsby** – The best choice for **static sites optimized for**

SEO.

With its server-first approach, progressive loading, and efficient rendering, Remix stands out as one of the best options for high-performance and interactive web applications.

MODULE 5: FRAMEWORKS FOR SERVERLESS AND EDGE COMPUTING – CLOUD EXECUTION

Serverless computing and the concept of edge computing have revolutionized the way applications are deployed, scaled, and distributed globally. In a world where latency and operational efficiency are critical to user experience, these paradigms allow applications to run without the need to manage traditional servers, leveraging the elasticity of the cloud and decentralized processing.

This module explores technologies that facilitate this transition, enabling the implementation of **scalable and high-performance solutions**. One of the highlights is the **Serverless Framework**, a tool that simplifies the creation and management of serverless applications, allowing developers to deploy code directly to providers such as **AWS Lambda, Google Cloud Functions, and Azure Functions**, without the traditional complexity of infrastructure management.

Additionally, specialized platforms like **Vercel** and **Netlify** have gained popularity by offering **optimized workflows for deploying modern web applications**. With support for **Server-Side Rendering (SSR) and edge functions**, these solutions enable applications to load with maximum efficiency, distributing processing to servers closer to end users.

For those looking for an **integrated solution directly with**

AWS, **AWS Amplify** stands out by providing a **complete set of tools** for **frontend and mobile application development and hosting**. With support for **GraphQL, storage, authentication, and CI/CD**, Amplify significantly reduces the complexity involved in building cloud-based applications.

Finally, an innovative approach for executing JavaScript and TypeScript on the edge is Deno Deploy, a platform that combines the simplicity of Deno with globally distributed execution, eliminating the need for conventional server configuration.

Throughout this module, each of these frameworks will be analyzed in depth, covering fundamental concepts, installation and configuration processes, key features, recommended use cases, practical demonstrations, common challenges, and best practices for optimization. Comparisons between these tools will also be made, assisting in choosing the best solution for different scenarios.

CHAPTER 31 – SERVERLESS FRAMEWORK

Serverless Framework is a tool that simplifies the creation, deployment, and management of serverless applications on cloud providers such as **AWS Lambda**, **Google Cloud Functions,** and **Azure Function**s. Its primary goal is to automate repetitive tasks, abstract infrastructure complexity, and provide an efficient workflow for developers who want to build highly scalable applications without managing traditional servers.

By using Serverless Framework, the entire application infrastructure can be defined through configuration files, ensuring reproducibility and ease of maintenance. Additionally, it allows the development of event-driven applications, where functions are executed only when triggered by specific events, reducing operational costs and optimizing resources.

Key advantages of Serverless Framework include:

- Unified management for multiple cloud providers.
- Support for various languages, such as JavaScript, Python, Go, and Java.
- Automated deployment with a single command.
- Easy integration with databases, queues, and APIs.
- Cost reduction by eliminating idle servers.

With this approach, companies and developers can focus on business logic and code without worrying about server maintenance or infrastructure scalability.

Installation and Basic Configuration

To install Serverless Framework, Node.js must be installed on the system. The installation can be done via npm with the following command:

bash

```
npm install -g serverless
```

After installation, the installed version can be verified by running:

bash

```
serverless -v
```

To create a new Serverless project, use:

bash

```
serverless create --template aws-nodejs --path my-application
cd my-application
npm install
```

This command generates a basic structure for a serverless application based on Node.js, already configured for deployment on AWS Lambda.

The main project file is **serverless.yml**, where the application's functions and settings are defined. A basic configuration example:

yaml

```
service: my-application
provider:
  name: aws
  runtime: nodejs18.x
```

```
functions:
  hello:
    handler: handler.hello
    events:
      - http:
          path: hello
          method: get
```

This configuration creates a function named hello, which will be triggered by an HTTP GET request at the /hello route.

To deploy the application to AWS Lambda, run:

bash

```
serverless deploy
```

The command returns the endpoint URL, allowing the function to be tested directly via a browser or **curl**:

bash

```
curl  https://xyz.execute-api.us-east-1.amazonaws.com/dev/
hello
```

Key Features and Differentiators

Serverless Framework offers several functionalities that make serverless application implementation more efficient, such as:

- Multi-cloud support, allowing use with AWS, Google Cloud, Azure, among others.
- Plugins and extensions that add features like advanced logging, monitoring, and database integration.
- Simplified environment management, allowing secure configuration of environment variables and credentials.
- Integrated authentication and permissions, facilitating

authentication via AWS IAM and API Gateway.

- Local testing and debugging, enabling simulation of function calls before deployment.

These features make Serverless Framework a robust and practical solution for developing highly scalable, low-latency serverless applications.

Use Cases and When to Choose

Serverless Framework is ideal for applications that require scalability and operational efficiency. The main use cases include:

- **Serverless APIs**, where endpoints are triggered on demand without the need to maintain active servers.
- **Real-time event processing**, such as log analysis, notifications, and IoT integration.
- **Task automation**, executing functions on scheduled times via AWS EventBridge or cron jobs.
- **Chatbots and virtual assistants**, using serverless functions to process messages and integrate with AI services.
- **ETL and data processing**, where functions process and transform data before storing it in databases.

If the application requires continuous execution and persistent state, other solutions such as containers or managed services may be more suitable.

Practical Demonstration with Code
Creating a serverless REST API

To define a REST API that returns a welcome message, edit the handler.js file:

javascript

```
module.exports.hello = async (event) => {
  return {
```

```
    statusCode: 200,
    body: JSON.stringify({ message: "Welcome to Serverless
Framework!" }),
  };
};
```

Now, edit **serverless.yml** to configure an HTTP endpoint:

yaml

```yaml
functions:
  hello:
    handler: handler.hello
    events:
      - http:
          path: hello
          method: get
```

Deploy the function with:

bash

```bash
serverless deploy
```

To test it, run:

bash

```bash
curl https://xyz.execute-api.us-east-1.amazonaws.com/dev/
hello
```

The expected output:

json

```json
{"message": "Welcome to Serverless Framework!"}
```

Adding Environment Variables

In **serverless.yml**, environment variables can be defined:

yaml

```
provider:
  environment:
    API_KEY: "123456"
```

Inside the function, variables can be accessed via **process.env**:

javascript

```
const apiKey = process.env.API_KEY;
console.log(`API Key: ${apiKey}`);
```

Common Errors and How to Fix Them

Error: "Missing credentials in config" when deploying to AWS

- **Cause:** AWS credentials not configured correctly.
- **Solution:** Configure credentials with **aws configure** or **serverless config credentials**.

Error: "Function not found" when calling HTTP endpoint

- **Cause:** The function was not deployed correctly.
- **Solution:** Check deployment logs with **serverless info** and redeploy with **serverless deploy**.

Error: "Access denied" when accessing a database or another service

- **Cause:** Insufficient permissions on AWS.
- **Solution:** Ensure the function has appropriate permissions in IAM.

Best Practices and Optimization

To optimize serverless applications, it is recommended to:

- **Minimize execution time**, ensuring functions execute only necessary tasks.
- **Use logging and monitoring**, to track errors and optimize performance.
- **Configure appropriate timeouts**, avoiding unnecessarily long executions.
- **Reduce function size**, eliminating unnecessary dependencies for faster initialization times.

Alternatives and Competing Frameworks

Serverless Framework competes with other solutions for serverless application development, such as:

- **AWS CDK** – An alternative for infrastructure as code on AWS.
- **Google Cloud Functions Framework** – A solution specifically for Google Cloud.
- **Architect** – A simplified framework for serverless applications.

With its flexibility, multi-cloud support, and large community, Serverless Framework stands out as one of the best options for agile and scalable development in the serverless computing era.

CHAPTER 32 – VERCEL

Vercel is a serverless deployment and hosting platform designed to deliver maximum performance for **modern applications**, especially those built with **Next.js, React, Vue.js, and Svelte.** Its main advantage is the combination of ease of use, automatic scalability, and edge computing support, ensuring fast loading and efficient application distribution worldwide.

By eliminating the need to configure servers or manage complex infrastructure, Vercel allows developers to focus on writing code while handling deployment, caching, and optimization through its global distribution network. The system is built to provide low latency, native support for SSR (Server-Side Rendering), and advanced functionalities such as Edge Functions, which process requests on servers closest to users.

Vercel's main objectives include:

- Providing an optimized hosting environment for modern frontend frameworks.
- Enabling continuous deployment with direct integration to GitHub, GitLab, and Bitbucket.
- Ensuring automatic scalability without requiring infrastructure management.
- Allowing edge code execution to reduce latency for global users.
- Integrating performance and SEO enhancements directly into the framework structure, optimizing websites and applications.

With its architecture focused on performance and simplicity,

Vercel is the ideal choice for developers looking for an agile and efficient workflow without sacrificing flexibility and high availability.

Installation and Basic Configuration

Vercel can be used directly via its web interface, but its true potential is revealed with the CLI (Command Line Interface), which allows developers to manage projects quickly and efficiently. To install the CLI, run:

bash

```
npm install -g vercel
```

After installation, authentication with a Vercel account is required:

bash

```
vercel login
```

Deploying a project is straightforward. Simply navigate to the project directory and run:

bash

```
vercel
```

The tool will automatically detect the framework in use and configure the appropriate environment. To manually define a project, use:

bash

```
vercel init
```

This command allows you to create a new Vercel project with

custom options.

Advanced configurations can be specified in the **vercel.json** file, where rules for routing, builds, and environment variables can be defined. A basic example:

json

```json
{
  "version": 2,
  "builds": [{ "src": "index.js", "use": "@vercel/node" }],
  "routes": [{ "src": "/(.*)", "dest": "/index.js" }]
}
```

This configuration directs all requests to **index.js**, where the backend logic is executed.

After setting up the project, deployment is done with a single command:

bash

```bash
vercel deploy
```

Vercel automatically provisions a free domain and makes the application available immediately.

Key Features and Differentiators

Vercel's key differentiator is its integration with frontend frameworks and the ability to execute code at the edge, drastically reducing response times. Its main features include:

- Native support for Next.js, including SSR, SSG, and ISR.
- Execution of functions at the edge, improving performance and security.
- Automatic Git-based deployment with version control integration.
- Global CDN ensuring reduced load times in any region.

- Incremental revalidation support, allowing dynamic updates without full recompilation.
- Preloading pages and image optimization, reducing load times.

With these features, Vercel is widely used by startups, large enterprises, and independent developers to build fast, scalable, and highly performant applications.

Use Cases and When to Choose

Vercel is ideal for serverless applications and modern frameworks, particularly when fast loading and efficient edge execution are required. Some of the primary use cases include:

- **SEO-optimized websites and blogs**, ensuring reduced load times.
- **Enterprise applications**, requiring high performance and low global latency.
- **E-commerce platforms**, where user experience and conversion rates depend on speed.
- **Interactive dashboards**, needing SSR and dynamic data updates.
- **Scalable APIs**, leveraging edge functions for rapid responses.

If greater control over infrastructure and deep customization are required, alternatives such as AWS Amplify or Netlify may be considered.

Practical Demonstration with Code

Deploying a Next.js Project on Vercel

Create a new Next.js project with:

bash

```
npx create-next-app@latest my-project
cd my-project
```

Log in to Vercel:

bash

vercel login

Now deploy the project with a single command:

bash

vercel

Vercel will automatically detect that it is a Next.js project and configure the best hosting options.

Creating an API on Vercel

To add a backend endpoint, create a file in **pages/api/hello.js** with the following content:

javascript

```
export default function handler(req, res) {
  res.status(200).json({ message: "API running on Vercel!" });
}
```

Now, deploy with:

bash

vercel deploy

The API will be immediately available at the generated Vercel URL.

Common Errors and How to Fix Them

Error: "Command not found: vercel"

- **Cause:** CLI was not installed correctly.
- **Solution:** Run **npm install -g vercel** again.

Error: "Project not linked to a Vercel account"

- **Cause:** The project was not authenticated properly.
- **Solution:** Run **vercel login** and link the account.

Error: "Build failed due to missing dependencies"

- **Cause:** The project is missing necessary dependencies.
- **Solution:** Run **npm install** before deploying.

Best Practices and Optimization

To achieve the best performance and security on Vercel, it is recommended to:

- **Enable edge caching**, reducing global load times.
- **Use environment variables**, preventing sensitive data exposure.
- **Minimize JavaScript on the client**, improving performance on mobile devices.
- **Leverage incremental revalidation**, ensuring pages update without full recompilation.
- **Monitor load time metrics**, ensuring an optimized user experience.

Alternatives and Competing Frameworks

Vercel is a leading platform in its segment, but it has direct competitors such as:

- **Netlify** – A serverless alternative with native Jamstack support and custom functions.
- **AWS Amplify** – Amazon's solution with greater flexibility but a more complex configuration.
- **Cloudflare Pages** – Ideal for hosting in edge computing with integrated CDN.

With its intuitive workflow, Git integration, and advanced Next.js support, Vercel stands out as one of the best platforms for developers seeking speed and scalability without compromising simplicity.

CHAPTER 33 – NETLIFY

Netlify is a modern **deployment and hosting platform designed for static sites**, web applications, and serverless services. Its primary goal is to provide a streamlined experience for developers by automating the entire project lifecycle, from continuous deployment to automatic scaling, without requiring complex server or infrastructure configuration.

Unlike traditional hosting approaches, Netlify combines **CDN (Content Delivery Network)**, serverless functions, and Git integration, ensuring performance, security, and ease of deployment. Additionally, the platform stands out for its support of **Jamstack (JavaScript, APIs, and Markup)**, an architectural model that enhances the user experience by reducing reliance on monolithic servers.

Key benefits of Netlify include:

- Simplified workflow with automatic deployments from Git repositories.
- Global distribution network (CDN), ensuring fast loading worldwide.
- Support for serverless functions, enabling dynamic backends without dedicated servers.
- Deployment previews, allowing changes to be tested before applying them to production.
- Automatic performance optimization, including file compression and intelligent caching.

With these features, Netlify has transformed how modern web applications are deployed, allowing developers to focus on code and user experience while the platform manages scalability and security.

Installation and Basic Configuration

A project can be deployed to Netlify directly through its web interface by linking a GitHub, GitLab, or Bitbucket repository, or by using the CLI (Command Line Interface) for terminal-based management.

Installing the Netlify CLI

For command-line use, install the CLI via npm:

bash

```
npm install -g netlify-cli
```

After installation, log in to your Netlify account with:

bash

```
netlify login
```

Creating a New Project

To create a new project by linking a Git repository, run:

bash

```
netlify init
```

This guided command allows selecting an existing project or creating a new one with the desired hosting structure.

Deploying an Application

If the application is already configured, simply run:

bash

```
netlify deploy
```

This generates a temporary link for project preview. To make it publicly accessible, use:

bash

```
netlify deploy --prod
```

This workflow enables any project to be deployed quickly without manual configurations or complex adjustments.

Key Features and Differentiators

Netlify goes beyond simple hosting by providing advanced tools that optimize development and application performance. Its main features include:

- Continuous deployment, automatically integrating with Git repositories for instant publishing.
- Branch previews, allowing changes to be tested before final publication.
- URL redirections and rewrites, simplifying routing without additional backend configuration.
- Netlify Functions, enabling serverless code execution without dedicated infrastructure.
- Edge Handlers, allowing processing at the edge to improve performance and request security.

These capabilities make Netlify one of the most comprehensive solutions for developers seeking simplicity and efficiency in web application deployment.

Use Cases and When to Choose

Netlify is particularly suited for projects that require high performance and easy deployment, including:

- **Static sites and blogs**, optimized for SEO and instant loading.
- **Portfolios and landing pages**, where speed and

simplicity are essential.

- **Jamstack-based applications**, leveraging APIs and dynamic frontend rendering.
- **Internal systems**, benefiting from branch previews and automated deployments.
- **Static e-commerce**, where user experience depends on fast response times.

If a more robust backend or advanced infrastructure control is needed, platforms like AWS Amplify or Vercel might be more appropriate.

Practical Demonstration with Code

Creating and Deploying a Static HTML Site

Create a folder with HTML, CSS, and JavaScript files:

bash

```
mkdir my-site
cd my-site
echo "<h1>Welcome to Netlify</h1>" > index.html
```

Now, run:

bash

```
netlify init
netlify deploy
```

This generates a temporary preview link. To make it permanent:

bash

```
netlify deploy --prod
```

The site will be immediately available on a Netlify-generated domain.

Creating a Serverless Function on Netlify

In Netlify, backend functions can be created directly inside the netlify/functions/ folder. Create a file called hello.js:

javascript

```javascript
exports.handler = async () => {
  return {
    statusCode: 200,
    body: JSON.stringify({ message: "API running on Netlify!" }),
  };
};
```

Now, edit **netlify.toml** to define the function:

toml

```toml
[build]
  functions = "netlify/functions"
```

Deploy the function:

bash

```bash
netlify deploy
```

The API will be automatically available at:

bash

```bash
https://my-site.netlify.app/.netlify/functions/hello
```

Common Errors and How to Fix Them

Error: "Command not found: netlify"

- **Cause:** CLI not installed correctly.
- **Solution:** Run **npm install -g netlify-cli** again.

Error: "Failed to connect repository"

- **Cause:** Failure to connect to a GitHub or GitLab repository.
- **Solution:** Reauthenticate with **netlify login** and check permissions.

Error: "Function not found" when calling a serverless function

- **Cause:** Function not deployed correctly.
- **Solution:** Verify the **netlify/functions/** folder structure and redeploy with **netlify deploy**.

Best Practices and Optimization

To ensure the best performance and security with Netlify, consider:

- **Using intelligent caching**, reducing load times for static files.
- **Configuring redirections and rewrites**, improving SEO and user experience.
- **Enabling JWT authentication** for serverless functions to ensure secure communication.
- **Minimizing JavaScript on the frontend**, improving response times.
- **Utilizing branch previews**, ensuring changes are tested before final deployment.

Alternatives and Competing Frameworks

Netlify is a leading modern deployment solution but has direct competitors such as:

- **Vercel** – A serverless alternative focused on SSR and edge computing, ideal for Next.js projects.
- **AWS Amplify** – A more flexible option for applications

integrated with AWS services.

- **Cloudflare Pages** – A superior choice for performance and security with edge computing capabilities.

With its intuitive workflow, native Git integration, and advanced serverless function support, Netlify stands out as one of the best platforms for developers seeking ease and efficiency in modern web application deployment.

CAPÍTULO 34 – AWS AMPLIFY

AWS Amplify is a framework and set of tools developed by **Amazon Web Services** to simplify the creation, deployment, and scalability of cloud-based web and mobile applications. Designed for frontend and mobile developers, it streamlines integration with AWS services, allowing applications to use authentication, databases, storage, APIs, and hosting with ease.

Its goal is to reduce infrastructure complexity by providing a declarative approach to configuring and managing cloud services. AWS Amplify enables development teams to focus on creating rich and dynamic user experiences without dealing directly with AWS's detailed configurations.

Key differentiators of Amplify include:

- Native integration with AWS, offering immediate support for services such as Cognito, DynamoDB, API Gateway, Lambda, and S3.
- Backend and frontend tools, allowing full-stack application development without manually setting up servers.
- Support for multiple frameworks, including React, Vue.js, Angular, Next.js, and Flutter.
- Continuous deployment and CI/CD integration, syncing changes directly from Git repositories.
- Support for serverless and edge computing applications, ensuring automatic scalability.

With these capabilities, AWS Amplify positions itself as a robust solution for developers looking for fast implementation and seamless integration with the AWS ecosystem.

Installation and Basic Configuration

To use AWS Amplify, Node.js must be installed. The CLI installation is done with:

bash

```
npm install -g @aws-amplify/cli
```

After installation, configure the CLI by authenticating your AWS account:

bash

```
amplify configure
```

This command starts a guided process that prompts for login and permission setup for AWS.

Creating a New Project

To start a project with AWS Amplify, navigate to the project directory and run:

bash

```
amplify init
```

The initialization process asks for information such as:

- Project name
- Environment (default: "dev")
- Platform (JavaScript, iOS, Android)
- AWS region
- Authentication setup

After configuration, AWS Amplify creates files in the project to store backend structure, allowing AWS services to be managed directly from the code.

Adding Features to the Project

Amplify allows adding backend features with simple commands. To include authentication via AWS Cognito, use:

bash

```
amplify add auth
```

To configure a NoSQL database with Amazon DynamoDB, use:

bash

```
amplify add storage
```

To create a GraphQL API with AWS AppSync, run:

bash

```
amplify add api
```

After adding the desired services, deploy the infrastructure to AWS by executing:

bash

```
amplify push
```

This creates the necessary resources and makes the application available for frontend integration.

Key Features and Differentiators

AWS Amplify stands out by offering deep integration with AWS, enabling developers to build complete applications without manually configuring each service. Key features include:

- Automated backend management, allowing

configuration and updates without using the AWS Console.

- Integrated authentication, supporting login via AWS Cognito, Facebook, Google, and Apple ID.
- Scalable APIs, supporting REST and GraphQL with automatic database resolution.
- Secure file storage, facilitating media uploads and management via S3.
- Continuous deployment via Git, automating application updates in production.
- Support for hybrid and mobile applications, integrating with React Native, iOS, and Android.

These differentiators make Amplify a powerful solution for developers looking to build modern cloud applications with minimal manual configuration.

Use Cases and When to Choose

AWS Amplify is ideal for frontend developers and teams looking to build full-stack applications without managing servers. Some primary use cases include:

- **Enterprise applications**, with secure authentication and scalable databases.
- **Dashboards and admin systems**, integrating real-time data.
- **E-commerce and marketplaces**, ensuring high availability and payment integration.
- **Hybrid mobile applications**, supporting push notifications and remote storage.
- **Educational platforms**, offering secure login and user management.

If the project requires advanced customization or granular infrastructure control, alternatives such as AWS CDK or Terraform may be more suitable.

Practical Demonstration with Code

Creating a Backend with Authentication

After initializing the project, add authentication:

bash

```
amplify add auth
```

Choose the desired options in the interactive menu, then deploy:

bash

```
amplify push
```

In the frontend, install the Amplify package:

bash

```
npm install aws-amplify @aws-amplify/ui-react
```

Now, configure authentication in **index.js**:

javascript

```
import { Amplify } from 'aws-amplify';
import awsconfig from './aws-exports';
import { withAuthenticator } from '@aws-amplify/ui-react';

Amplify.configure(awsconfig);

function App() {
  return <h1>Authentication with AWS Amplify</h1>;
}

export default withAuthenticator(App);
```

With this setup, the application will be integrated with AWS Cognito and allow secure login.

Creating a GraphQL API

Add a GraphQL API to the project:

bash

```
amplify add api
```

Choose GraphQL and the initial schema. After configuration, deploy the API:

bash

```
amplify push
```

To query data from the frontend, use the GraphQL package:

javascript

```javascript
import { API, graphqlOperation } from 'aws-amplify';
import { listPosts } from './graphql/queries';

async function fetchPosts() {
  const posts = await
API.graphql(graphqlOperation(listPosts));
  console.log(posts);
}
```

This allows data to be retrieved from the database automatically.

Common Errors and How to Fix Them

Error: "User is not authorized to perform this action"

- **Cause:** Insufficient permissions in Cognito or IAM.
- **Solution:** Check permissions in the AWS console.

Error: "API key expired" when calling GraphQL

- **Cause:** The default API key has a limited validity.
- **Solution:** Run amplify update api and update permissions.

Error: "Failed to push resources" when deploying the backend

- **Cause:** Schema version conflict.
- **Solution:** Run amplify status and verify if there are unapplied changes.

Best Practices and Optimization

To ensure better performance and security when using AWS Amplify, follow these recommendations:

- **Configure proper permissions**, ensuring that only authorized users access sensitive resources.
- **Optimize the GraphQL API**, using paginated queries to avoid excessive data consumption.
- **Monitor logs via CloudWatch**, identifying errors and performance bottlenecks.
- **Use Git repositories for version control**, ensuring safe rollback in case of failures.
- **Leverage caching and efficient storage**, minimizing costs and loading times.

Alternatives and Competing Frameworks

AWS Amplify competes with various solutions for full-stack and serverless development, such as:

- **Vercel** – Ideal for frontend applications with edge computing.
- **Netlify** – Focused on continuous deployment and simplified infrastructure.

- **Firebase** – Google's alternative with real-time databases and simplified authentication.

With its native AWS integration, full-stack support, and automatic scalability, Amplify stands out as one of the best options for building robust cloud applications with minimal operational complexity.

CHAPTER 35 – DENO DEPLOY

Deno Deploy is a serverless platform that allows **JavaScript, TypeScript, and WebAssembly** code execution directly at the **network edge (edge computing)** without the need to manage servers. It was designed to offer ultra-fast response times, enhanced security, and native integration with the Deno runtime.

Unlike Node.js, Deno comes with built-in support for TypeScript, secure dependencies without the need for package managers, and a permissions model that prevents unrestricted access to the file system and network. With Deno Deploy, applications can be globally distributed, reducing latency for users anywhere.

Key benefits of Deno Deploy include:

- Execution at the Edge, ensuring low latency worldwide.
- Support for modern JavaScript and TypeScript without manual compilation.
- Integrated security model, preventing unauthorized access to system resources.
- Continuous deployment with direct integration to Git repositories.
- Native serverless execution, eliminating the need for complex infrastructure configuration.

These features make Deno Deploy an excellent alternative for developers who need fast code distribution, advanced security, and automatic scalability.

Installation and Basic Configuration

To use Deno Deploy, the first step is to install the Deno runtime on your local environment. This can be done via the terminal:

bash

curl -fsSL https://deno.land/install.sh | sh

After installation, verify that Deno is available by running:

bash

deno --version

With the runtime installed, applications can be created and tested locally before deploying to the serverless platform.

Creating a Project with Deno Deploy

To start a basic project, create a **server.ts** file with the following code:

typescript

```
import { serve } from "https://deno.land/std@0.200.0/http/
server.ts";

serve((req) => new Response("Deno Deploy is active!", { status:
200 }), { port: 8000 });
```

This code creates a basic HTTP server that responds with "Deno Deploy is active!" to all requests.

Deploying to the Cloud with Deno Deploy

Deno Deploy provides a web interface for instant deployment. To deploy the code:

1. Access Deno Deploy Dashboard.
2. Create a new project.
3. Upload the **server.ts** file or connect to a Git repository.

4. The code will be automatically distributed across the global edge computing network.

The deployment can be automatically updated by integrating with Git repositories, ensuring that any changes in the code are quickly reflected in production.

Key Features and Differentiators

Deno Deploy provides a modern approach to serverless execution, with key features such as:

- **Cloud-optimized runtime**, enabling fast and efficient execution.
- **Native support for ES6 modules**, eliminating the need for NPM packages.
- **Integration with WebAssembly**, allowing high-performance code execution.
- **Edge Computing execution**, reducing global latency.
- **Secure and isolated APIs**, preventing unauthorized access to the file system.
- **Controlled permissions model**, explicitly defining which resources can be accessed.

These functionalities make Deno Deploy a highly efficient solution for modern applications that require fast response times and enhanced security.

Use Cases and When to Choose

Deno Deploy is ideal for projects that require low latency, automatic scalability, and enhanced security, such as:

- **Serverless APIs**, optimized for edge execution.
- **Jamstack websites and applications**, ensuring instant loading.
- **Automation and backend scripts**, without the need for dedicated servers.
- **Real-time data streaming services**, where response time is critical.

- **WebAssembly (WASM) execution**, enabling complex computational tasks.

If the goal is traditional backend execution or broader NPM package support, alternatives like AWS Lambda or Vercel may be more suitable.

Practical Demonstration with Code

Creating a Serverless REST API

To create a basic REST API with Deno Deploy, create the **api.ts** file:

typescript

```typescript
import { serve } from "https://deno.land/std@0.200.0/http/server.ts";

const handler = (req: Request): Response => {
  return new Response(JSON.stringify({ message: "Serverless API with Deno Deploy!" }), {
    headers: { "Content-Type": "application/json" },
  });
};

serve(handler, { port: 8080 });
```

Now, deploy via **Deno Deploy Dashboard**, and the API will be available at a public URL.

Running WebAssembly on Deno Deploy

Deno Deploy supports WebAssembly (WASM) execution. To run WASM code, create the **wasm.ts** file:

typescript

```typescript
const wasmCode = new Uint8Array([
  0x00, 0x61, 0x73, 0x6d, 0x01, 0x00, 0x00, 0x00,
```

```
  // WebAssembly binary code here
]);

const wasmModule = await
WebAssembly.compile(wasmCode);
const instance = await
WebAssembly.instantiate(wasmModule);

console.log("Executing WASM on Deno Deploy", instance);
```

This script enables applications to perform high-performance computations in the cloud.

Common Errors and How to Fix Them

Error: "Module not found" when importing packages

- **Cause:** Deno does not use a package manager like NPM.
- **Solution:** Ensure imports use direct URLs, such as https://deno.land/std/http/server.ts.

Error: "Permission denied" when accessing files

- **Cause:** Deno's security model prevents unauthorized access to the system.
- **Solution:** Run the script locally with the --allow-read flag:

bash

```
deno run --allow-read file.ts
```

Error: "Failed to deploy" when uploading code to the cloud

- **Cause:** The code contains imports not supported by Deno Deploy.
- **Solution:** Use only modules compatible with Deno.

Best Practices and Optimization

To ensure optimal performance and security with Deno Deploy, follow these recommendations:

- **Use Deno standard modules**, avoiding unnecessary dependencies.
- **Configure access permissions**, minimizing security risks.
- **Leverage serverless execution**, avoiding unnecessary persistent processes.
- **Distribute workloads across multiple endpoints**, ensuring efficient scalability.
- **Adjust cache lifetime and HTTP headers**, optimizing global performance.

Alternatives and Competing Frameworks

Deno Deploy competes with various serverless and edge computing platforms, such as:

- **Vercel Edge Functions** – Excellent for SSR with Next.js and reduced latency.
- **Cloudflare Workers** – A performance and security-focused alternative.
- **AWS Lambda** – A scalable option but with more complex configuration.

With its modern architecture, native TypeScript support, and edge computing execution, Deno Deploy stands out as one of the best choices for developers seeking high performance and security without complexity.

MODULE 6: FRAMEWORKS FOR SECURITY AND AUTHENTICATION – PROTECTION AND ACCESS MANAGEMENT

Security in web development is one of the fundamental pillars for ensuring the integrity, confidentiality, and availability of modern systems. With the increasing use of distributed applications, publicly exposed APIs, and the need for efficient authentication, specialized frameworks play a critical role in protecting sensitive data and mitigating cybersecurity threats.

This module presents the main frameworks for security and authentication, covering solutions that facilitate identity management, access control, and robust security policies. Each explored framework offers different approaches to ensure that users and services are authenticated securely, in addition to providing features for permission management, regulatory compliance, and protection against common attacks such as brute force and credential injection.

The journey begins with **Auth.js**, a versatile framework that enables modular authentication implementation in web applications, supporting identity providers such as Google, GitHub, and Facebook. Next, **Keycloak** is introduced as a comprehensive identity and access management solution, allowing **Single Sign-On (SSO)** and granular permission control for enterprise applications.

The module then explores **Supabase Auth**, an authentication service that combines ease of use with direct integration into PostgreSQL databases, providing **JWT-based authentication** and **OAuth** support. Complementing this approach, **Ory** brings a modern architecture for identity control, offering flexible APIs to manage authentication, authorization, and compliance with standards such as **OpenID Connect**.

Finally, **policy-based security** is covered with **Open Policy Agent (OPA)**, a powerful framework that allows defining and enforcing authorization rules declaratively, promoting a secure and centralized model for access decisions in **microservices** and distributed applications.

Throughout this module, each of these frameworks will be explored in detail, highlighting their **key features, use cases, and practical implementation**. The choice of the ideal solution will depend on the level of control needed over authentication and authorization, the degree of integration with other services, and the complexity of the application. With this approach, developers and software architects will gain the necessary knowledge to **strengthen application security and ensure efficient identity and access management**.

CHAPTER 36 – AUTH.JS

Authentication is one of the fundamental pillars of security in web applications, ensuring that only authorized users have access to functionalities and sensitive data. **Auth.js** is a modular and flexible authentication library designed to simplify the implementation of secure login in modern web applications.

Unlike monolithic solutions, Auth.js focuses on flexibility and scalability, allowing developers to integrate multiple identity providers such as **Google, GitHub, Facebook, Apple**, and traditional credential-based authentication (email/password) with support for **JWT (JSON Web Tokens)**.

Its primary purpose is to simplify integration with authentication providers and provide a consistent API for managing login, logout, sessions, and account recovery. Some of Auth.js's key features include:

- **Support for multiple providers** – Easy integration with **OAuth, OpenID Connect, Magic Links**, and traditional authentication.
- **Unified and secure API** – Full control over sessions, **token-based authentication**, and **protected cookies**.
- **Compatibility with Next.js** – Native integration with **server-side applications**, eliminating the need for a separate backend.
- **Advanced security** – Protection against **replay attacks, CSRF**, and efficient **session management**.

With these features, Auth.js is one of the best options for implementing **modern, secure, and scalable** authentication.

Installation and basic configuration

The initial setup of Auth.js depends on the environment in which it will be used. In **Next.js applications**, it can be installed with the following command:

bash

```
npm install next-auth
```

After installation, create an auth.ts file inside the **Next.js API** directory:

typescript

```
import NextAuth from "next-auth";
import Providers from "next-auth/providers";

export default NextAuth({
  providers: [
    Providers.Google({
      clientId: process.env.GOOGLE_CLIENT_ID,
      clientSecret: process.env.GOOGLE_CLIENT_SECRET,
    }),
  ],
});
```

This configuration enables **Google OAuth authentication**, using credentials stored in **environment variables**. To allow users to log in, add the following frontend code:

typescript

```
import { signIn, signOut, useSession } from "next-auth/react";

function AuthButton() {
```

```
const { data: session } = useSession();

return session ? (
  <button onClick={() => signOut()}>Sign out</button>
) : (
  <button onClick={() => signIn("google")}>Sign in with
Google</button>
);
}

export default AuthButton;
```

This allows users to log in and out seamlessly, with **automatic session management**.

Key features and differentiators

Auth.js provides various functionalities to enhance security and authentication flexibility in web applications:

- **Session management** – Allows users to stay authenticated with **secure tokens stored via cookies**.
- **Social authentication** – Native support for providers such as **Google, GitHub, Twitter, Apple, and Facebook**.
- **JWT and protected cookies** – Enhanced security against **session attacks**.
- **Passwordless login via Magic Links** – A user-friendly alternative to traditional authentication.
- **Multiple authentication strategies** – Supports OAuth, **database-based authentication**, and **WebAuthn**.

These features make Auth.js a highly flexible solution for applications requiring modern and secure authentication.

Use cases and when to choose

Auth.js is recommended for web applications that require robust and flexible authentication without a dedicated backend. Some ideal scenarios include:

- **SaaS platforms**, where users authenticate using different providers.
- **E-commerce and marketplaces**, ensuring **secure customer login**.
- **Enterprise systems**, with **Single Sign-On (SSO)** support.
- **Serverless applications**, where identity management needs to be handled without a persistent backend.

If granular permission control and authorization management are required, frameworks like Keycloak or Ory might be better suited.

Practical demonstration with code

Configuring authentication via GitHub

To add **GitHub authentication**, update the Auth.js configuration:

typescript

```typescript
import NextAuth from "next-auth";
import GitHubProvider from "next-auth/providers/github";

export default NextAuth({
  providers: [
    GitHubProvider({
      clientId: process.env.GITHUB_CLIENT_ID,
      clientSecret: process.env.GITHUB_CLIENT_SECRET,
    }),
  ],
});
```

On the frontend, add the login button:

typescript

```
<button onClick={() => signIn("github")}>Sign in with
GitHub</button>
```

Now, users can authenticate using their **GitHub credentials**.

Implementing JWT authentication

If **JWT authentication** is required, configure it in auth.ts:

typescript

```
export default NextAuth({
  session: {
    strategy: "jwt",
  },
});
```

Now, sessions will be managed via JSON Web Tokens, enabling integration with external APIs.

Common errors and how to solve them

Error: "Provider not configured" when trying to authenticate

- **Cause:** The provider was not properly configured.
- **Solution:** Ensure the **provider credentials** are correctly set in the environment.

Error: "Invalid callback URL" in OAuth login

- **Cause:** The identity provider does not recognize the redirect URL.
- **Solution:** Configure the **correct callback URL** in the provider's dashboard (Google, GitHub, etc.).

Error: "Session expired" when trying to retrieve a session

- **Cause:** The JWT expiration time is too short.
- **Solution:** Adjust the token duration in the Auth.js configuration:

typescript

```
export default NextAuth({
  jwt: {
    maxAge: 60 * 60 * 24, // 24 hours
  },
});
```

Best practices and optimization

To enhance performance and security when using Auth.js, follow these recommendations:

- **Store credentials securely** – Use **environment variables** for API keys.
- **Implement multi-factor authentication (MFA)** – Increases security by requiring a second authentication factor.
- **Use JWT only when necessary** – For **backend-dedicated** applications, **cookie-based sessions** are more secure.
- **Automatically revoke inactive sessions** – Set an **expiration time** for sessions, reducing risks of unauthorized access.

Alternatives and competing frameworks

Auth.js competes with various authentication solutions, including:

- **Firebase Authentication** – A good alternative for those needing a **managed backend with built-in authentication**.
- **Keycloak** – Suitable for **SSO (Single Sign-On)** and **fine-grained permission control**.
- **Ory Kratos** – Focused on **decentralized identity** and **advanced user control**.

With native support for multiple providers, flexibility, and ease of implementation, Auth.js stands out as one of the best choices for modern and secure authentication in web applications.

CHAPTER 37 – KEYCLOAK

Security in modern application development requires robust solutions for **user authentication and authorization**. **Keycloak** is an **Identity and Access Management (IAM) framework** that provides a **complete solution** for identity management and access control. It allows developers to implement **Single Sign-On (SSO), Multi-Factor Authentication (MFA), and advanced permission control** without the need to build authentication systems from scratch.

Developed by Red Hat, Keycloak is an open-source platform widely adopted in enterprise applications, distributed systems, and microservices, supporting OpenID Connect, OAuth 2.0, and SAML. Its primary purpose is to provide a centralized identity server, allowing different applications to share authentication without duplicating credential storage.

Some of **Keycloak's** key features include:

- **Centralized authentication and authorization** – Multiple applications can use the same identity server.
- **Single Sign-On (SSO)** – Users log in once and access multiple applications **without re-authenticating**.
- **Multi-Factor Authentication (MFA)** – Support for **One-Time Passwords (OTP)** and integration with authenticators.
- **Role-Based Access Control (RBAC) and Attribute-Based Access Control (ABAC) – Granular permission management** for users and groups.
- **Flexible administration** – A **full web interface** for managing users, policies, and authentication providers.

Due to its high configurability, Keycloak is widely used by large enterprises and systems that require advanced security and scalability.

Installation and Basic Configuration

Keycloak can be installed locally for testing or deployed in a production environment. It can be run using Docker, making its setup quick and efficient.

Installation via Docker

To run **Keycloak** with an **embedded database**, use:

bash

```
docker run -p 8080:8080 \
  -e KEYCLOAK_ADMIN=admin \
  -e KEYCLOAK_ADMIN_PASSWORD=admin \
  quay.io/keycloak/keycloak:latest \
  start-dev
```

After execution, the **administration panel** can be accessed at **http://localhost:8080** using the defined credentials **(admin/admin)**.

Initial Configuration

Once logged into the admin interface, the basic setup steps for integrating Keycloak into an application are:

1. **Create a new Realm** – A **Realm** in **Keycloak** is an **isolated instance** for managing users and authentication settings.
2. **Register a Client** – Applications using **Keycloak** must be **registered as clients**.
3. **Define Authentication Methods** – Choose from **user/password authentication, OAuth2.0, OpenID Connect, or SAML**.

4. **Create Users and Groups** – Manage **user profiles** and define **group permissions**.

With this basic configuration, Keycloak is ready for centralized authentication integration into applications.

Key Features and Differentiators

Keycloak stands out for its robust features and flexibility, making it one of the best options for businesses needing total control over authentication and authorization.

Among its **main features**, we highlight:

- **Single Sign-On (SSO)** – Users **log in once** and access multiple applications **without re-authenticating**.
- **Identity Brokering** – Integration with **external identity providers** such as **Google, GitHub, Microsoft, and LDAP**.
- **Support for Multiple Protocols** – Compatible with **OAuth2.0, OpenID Connect, and SAML**, ensuring flexibility for different scenarios.
- **Advanced Authorization** – **Detailed permission control** through **Role-Based Access Control (RBAC)** and **Attribute-Based Access Control (ABAC)**.
- **Administration and Auditing** – **A complete interface** for managing users, **sessions, and audit logs**.

These features make Keycloak one of the most complete and powerful identity frameworks available.

Use Cases and When to Choose

Keycloak is recommended for applications that require centralized identity control and robust authentication. It excels in the following scenarios:

- **Enterprises with multiple internal systems** requiring **secure SSO** to simplify employee login.
- **SaaS (Software as a Service) platforms** needing **secure authentication** and **multi-provider integration**.

- **Enterprise applications** requiring **advanced permission management** and compliance with **security standards**.
- **Microservices architectures** that need **centralized authentication**, using **OAuth2.0** for **secure service-to-service communication**.

If the goal is a simpler authentication solution, lighter frameworks like Auth.js or Firebase Authentication might be more suitable.

Practical Demonstration with Code

Setting Up OpenID Connect Authentication in a Node.js Application

To integrate **Keycloak** into a **Node.js application**, install the **keycloak-connect** library:

bash

```
npm install keycloak-connect express-session
```

In the **backend**, configure the **Keycloak middleware**:

javascript

```
const express = require('express');
const session = require('express-session');
const Keycloak = require('keycloak-connect');

const app = express();
const memoryStore = new session.MemoryStore();

const keycloak = new Keycloak({ store: memoryStore });

app.use(session({ secret: 'my-secret-key', resave: false,
saveUninitialized: true, store: memoryStore }));
app.use(keycloak.middleware());
```

```
app.get('/protected', keycloak.protect(), (req, res) => {
  res.send('Access granted');
});

app.listen(3000, () => console.log('Server running on port
3000'));
```

This code protects the /protected route, allowing only authenticated users in Keycloak to access it.

Common Errors and How to Resolve Them

Error: "Invalid redirect URI" when trying to authenticate

- **Cause:** The **redirect URL** was not configured correctly in **Keycloak**.
- **Solution:** In the **admin panel**, add the **correct redirect URL** in the **client configuration**.

Error: "Client not found" when trying to log in

- **Cause:** The **client ID** used in the application does not match any registered **Keycloak clients**.
- **Solution:** Verify the **client configuration** and ensure it is **active**.

Error: "403 Forbidden" when accessing a protected route

- **Cause:** The authenticated user **does not have permission** to access the resource.
- **Solution:** Define **correct permissions** in the **admin panel** by adding **roles to the user**.

Best Practices and Optimization

To ensure **maximum performance and security** when using **Keycloak**, follow these recommendations:

- **Enable Multi-Factor Authentication (MFA)** – Require a **second authentication factor** for additional security.

- **Manage sessions efficiently** – Use **Redis** or **databases** to store sessions in **distributed environments**.
- **Automatically revoke inactive sessions** – Set an **expiration time for tokens** and **inactive sessions**.
- **Monitor audit logs** – Use **Keycloak's built-in tools** to log login attempts and suspicious events.

Alternatives and Competing Frameworks

Keycloak competes with various identity management solutions, such as:

- **Auth0** – A **commercial alternative** with **easy integration**, but at a **higher cost**.
- **Okta** – **Focused on enterprises** needing **corporate authentication and regulatory compliance**.
- **Ory Kratos** – An **open-source alternative** for **decentralized identity** and **advanced user control**.

With multi-protocol support, advanced permission control, and a full administration interface, Keycloak stands out as one of the most powerful solutions for enterprise identity management and authentication.

CHAPTER 38 – SUPABASE AUTH

Authentication is a cornerstone of **security in web and mobile applications**, ensuring that only authorized users can access sensitive information. **Supabase Auth** is a **comprehensive and open-source authentication solution**, designed to provide **secure, scalable, and easy-to-implement authentication**.

Developed as an alternative to Firebase Authentication, Supabase Auth uses PostgreSQL as its backend and offers authentication via JWT-based tokens, OAuth, email/password authentication, magic links, and external providers. Its main advantage is native integration with relational databases, allowing identity management directly within the database without the need for intermediary servers.

Among its key features, Supabase Auth offers:

- **Support for multiple authentication methods**, including **OAuth, WebAuthn, and traditional authentication**.
- **Identity management based on Postgres**, ensuring **direct control over users and permissions**.
- **Secure JWT tokens**, allowing the creation of **protected APIs** without requiring a separate authentication server.
- **Webhooks for authentication events**, enabling **notifications and access monitoring**.
- **Fully open-source**, offering **transparency and flexibility** for developers who want **full control over their applications**.

Due to its seamless integration with Supabase Database, this framework is highly recommended for applications that use PostgreSQL as a backend.

Installation and Basic Configuration

Using Supabase Auth begins with creating a Supabase project. After signing up and accessing the dashboard, the next step is configuring authentication.

Installing the SDK in the Frontend

If you are using JavaScript or TypeScript, the first step is to install the Supabase SDK:

bash

```
npm install @supabase/supabase-js
```

Next, configure the **connection in the frontend**:

javascript

```
import { createClient } from '@supabase/supabase-js';

const supabase = createClient('https://YOUR_SUPABASE_URL', 'YOUR_SUPABASE_ANON_KEY');
```

With this configuration, users can be authenticated using **different methods.**

Enabling Authentication Providers

In the Supabase dashboard, navigate to the Auth tab and enable the desired providers, such as Google, GitHub, or Apple. Then, configure the API keys obtained from the respective platforms.

For **Google OAuth authentication**, for example, use:

javascript

```
const { user, error } = await supabase.auth.signInWithOAuth({
  provider: 'google',
```

```
});
```

If an error occurs during login, the error variable will contain detailed information about the failure.

Key Features and Differentiators

Supabase Auth stands out for its flexible and scalable approach, allowing developers to decide how and where to store credentials and user sessions.

Among its **main features**, we highlight:

- **Serverless authentication** – Since **it does not require a dedicated backend**, Supabase Auth **reduces the complexity** of implementing secure login.
- **Advanced permission control** – Thanks to **integration with PostgreSQL Row-Level Security (RLS)**, access rules can be defined **directly in the database**.
- **WebAuthn and MFA** – Supports **biometric authentication and multi-factor authentication** for increased security.
- **Signed JWT tokens** – Enables **authentication integration with REST and GraphQL APIs** without requiring server-side state.
- **Webhooks for login events** – Facilitates the **implementation of notifications, access auditing, and post-login actions**.

Use Cases and When to Choose

Supabase Auth is recommended for applications that require secure authentication based on a relational database. Some common use cases include:

- **Enterprise systems**, where authentication is directly tied to **database permissions**.
- **APIs protected by JWT**, where authentication needs to be **integrated into the endpoint authorization flow**.

- **SaaS platforms**, allowing users to use **social logins** without needing a separate identity server.
- **Applications using PostgreSQL**, leveraging the database's security and scalability.

If an application requires more complex identity management with granular permission control, frameworks like Keycloak or Ory Kratos may be better suited.

Practical Demonstration with Code

Implementing Email and Password Login

Email/password login in **Supabase Auth** is simple and direct:

javascript

```javascript
const { user, error } = await
supabase.auth.signInWithPassword({
  email: 'user@example.com',
  password: 'password123'
});

if (error) {
  console.error('Login error:', error.message);
} else {
  console.log('Authenticated user:', user);
}
```

If the user is not yet registered, an account can be created as follows:

javascript

```javascript
const { user, error } = await supabase.auth.signUp({
  email: 'user@example.com',
  password: 'password123'
});
```

Logging Out the User

To log out an **authenticated user**, use:

javascript

```
await supabase.auth.signOut();
```

This invalidates the active session and removes the authentication token.

Protecting Routes in a Node.js Backend

If the application includes a protected API, the JWT token can be verified in endpoints:

javascript

```
import express from 'express';
import { createClient } from '@supabase/supabase-js';

const app = express();
const supabase = createClient('https://YOUR_SUPABASE_URL',
'YOUR_SUPABASE_ANON_KEY');

app.use(express.json());

app.post('/api/protected', async (req, res) => {
  const token = req.headers.authorization?.split(' ')[1];

  const { data, error } = await supabase.auth.getUser(token);

  if (error || !data.user) {
    return res.status(401).json({ error: 'Access denied' });
  }

  res.json({ message: 'Access granted' });
```

```
});

app.listen(3000, () => console.log('API running on port 3000'));
```

Common Errors and How to Fix Them

Error: "Invalid API key" when trying to authenticate

- **Cause:** The API key **does not match the Supabase project settings**.
- **Solution:** Ensure the **correct API key is used** and that **allowed domains** include the application.

Error: "User not found" during login

- **Cause:** The **email entered is not registered** in the user database.
- **Solution:** Confirm that the user exists and that the **account has been properly verified**.

Error: "Session expired" when accessing a protected resource

- **Cause:** The **authentication token has expired or been revoked**.
- **Solution: Request a new login** to renew the JWT token.

Best Practices and Optimization

To enhance security and efficiency when using Supabase Auth, follow these recommendations:

- **Enable Multi-Factor Authentication (MFA) to strengthen security** for sensitive accounts.
- **Configure Row-Level Security (RLS) rules** in the database to **ensure users can only access their own data**.
- **Use short-lived tokens and refresh tokens** to improve the **user experience** without compromising security.
- **Enable audit logs** to **monitor login and logout events**.

Alternatives and Competing Frameworks

Supabase Auth competes with other authentication solutions, such as:

- **Firebase Authentication**, which provides a **managed backend** but has **less flexibility for PostgreSQL**.
- **Keycloak**, for **enterprises needing centralized authentication** and **granular user control**.
- **Auth0**, suitable for **enterprise applications** that require **multiple login methods** with **regulatory compliance**.

Thanks to its open-source approach, direct PostgreSQL integration, and support for multiple authentication methods, Supabase Auth establishes itself as one of the best choices for applications requiring secure and scalable authentication.

CAPÍTULO 39 – ORY

Digital identity security and access management are fundamental for any modern web application. **Ory** is an **open-source identity and authentication management platform**, designed for **scalable and secure applications**. It stands out for offering **flexible access control, robust authentication, and distributed session management**.

Unlike solutions like Firebase Auth and Supabase Auth, which focus on simplifying social login integration and basic authentication, Ory is designed for advanced identity control and customized authorization policies.

Main Components of Ory

Ory is composed of multiple **modular services**, each focused on a **specific security function**:

- **Ory Kratos – Identity and authentication management.**
- **Ory Hydra – OAuth2 and OpenID Connect implementation for Single Sign-On (SSO).**
- **Ory Keto – Policy-based access control system.**
- **Ory Oathkeeper – Authorization gateway for API protection.**

This modular architecture allows developers to implement multi-factor authentication (MFA), password recovery, profile management, access control, and SSO in a flexible and secure way.

Installation and Basic Configuration

The installation process for Ory depends on the specific component being used. For identity and authentication management, we use Ory Kratos.

Installing Ory Kratos

Ory Kratos can be installed locally or using Docker containers. For a quick setup with Docker, follow these steps:

Clone the Ory Kratos repository:

bash

```
git clone https://github.com/ory/kratos.git
cd kratos
```

Start the **Kratos services** along with the database:

bash

```
docker-compose up -d
```

This command starts Kratos, PostgreSQL, and an identity server pre-configured with basic authentication rules.

Check if Kratos is running properly:

bash

```
curl http://127.0.0.1:4433/health/alive
```

If everything is correct, the response will be a JSON object indicating that the service is active.

Creating an Authentication Flow

To authenticate a user, it is necessary to create a login flow. This can be done by calling the Ory Kratos API:

bash

```
curl -X GET "http://127.0.0.1:4433/self-service/login/api"
```

The response will contain a flow ID, which can be used to redirect users to the login form.

To authenticate a user **via API**, send the **credentials** to the **login endpoint**:

bash

```
curl -X POST "http://127.0.0.1:4433/self-service/login?
flow=<FLOW_ID>" \
  -H "Content-Type: application/json" \
  -d '{
    "identifier": "user@example.com",
    "password": "SecurePassword123"
  }'
```

If the credentials are correct, the user will be **authenticated** and receive a **session token**.

Key Features and Differentiators

Ory stands out for its granular identity and authorization control, allowing developers to define highly customized authentication rules.

Some of its **main features include**:

- **Advanced authentication** – Supports **multiple login methods**, including **email/password, SSO, passwordless authentication, and WebAuthn.**
- **Centralized access control** – Implements **RBAC (Role-Based Access Control)** and **ABAC (Attribute-Based Access Control).**
- **Session management** – Monitors **user access** and prevents **session hijacking.**
- **Multi-factor authentication (MFA)** – Native support for **TOTP, SMS authentication, and physical security**

devices.

- **OpenID Connect and OAuth2** – Integration with **external providers** for **federated authentication**.
- **Policy-based authorization** – With **Ory Keto**, developers can define **detailed access rules** for **APIs and internal systems**.

Use Cases and When to Choose

Ory is recommended for applications that require advanced authentication, identity management, and centralized access control.

Some of its common use cases include:

- **SaaS platforms** – Managing **thousands of users** with **detailed permission levels**.
- **APIs protected by OAuth2/OpenID** – Implementing **Single Sign-On (SSO)** and **distributed authorization control**.
- **Enterprise applications** – Requiring **multi-factor authentication** and **compliance with security standards** like **GDPR and HIPAA**.
- **Critical systems and fintechs** – Where **digital identity security** is an **essential factor**.

If an application requires a simpler authentication solution based on a database, frameworks like Supabase Auth or Firebase Authentication may be more suitable.

Practical Demonstration with Code

Implementing Login and Logout via API

To authenticate a user in a Node.js backend using Ory Kratos, we can use the following code:

javascript

```
import axios from 'axios';
```

```
const KRATOS_BASE_URL = 'http://127.0.0.1:4433';

async function login(email, password) {
  try {
    const { data } = await axios.post(`${KRATOS_BASE_URL}/
self-service/login?flow=<FLOW_ID>`, {
      identifier: email,
      password: password
    });

    console.log('Session started:', data.session_token);
  } catch (error) {
    console.error('Login error:', error.response?.data ||
error.message);
  }
}

async function logout(token) {
  try {
    await axios.delete(`${KRATOS_BASE_URL}/sessions`, {
      headers: { Authorization: `Bearer ${token}` }
    });

    console.log('Session ended.');
  } catch (error) {
    console.error('Logout error:', error.response?.data ||
error.message);
  }
}
```

Protecting Routes in an Express Backend

To verify if a user is **authenticated before accessing a**

protected endpoint, we can implement a **middleware**:

javascript

```javascript
async function verifySession(req, res, next) {
  const token = req.headers.authorization?.split(' ')[1];

  if (!token) {
    return res.status(401).json({ error: 'Authentication token missing' });
  }

  try {
    const { data } = await axios.get(`${KRATOS_BASE_URL}/sessions/whoami`, {
      headers: { Authorization: `Bearer ${token}` }
    });

    req.user = data;
    next();
  } catch (error) {
    res.status(401).json({ error: 'Invalid or expired session' });
  }
}
```

Common Errors and How to Fix Them

Error: "Missing or invalid flow ID" when trying to authenticate

- **Cause:** The **authentication flow ID** was not included in the request.
- **Solution:** Make sure to **obtain the flow ID before initiating authentication.**

Error: "Session not found" when verifying a user session

- **Cause:** The **authentication token has expired or was revoked.**
- **Solution: Request a new login** to refresh the user session.

Error: "Unauthorized" when accessing protected APIs

- **Cause:** The user **does not have permission** to access the requested resource.
- **Solution:** Configure **access rules** using **Ory Keto** to define **proper permissions.**

Best Practices and Optimization

- **Enable multi-factor authentication (MFA)** to **enhance user security.**
- **Monitor active sessions** to detect **suspicious access patterns.**
- **Set token expiration policies** to **prevent unnecessary prolonged sessions.**
- **Use audit logs** to **track login attempts and authentication failures.**

Alternatives and Competing Frameworks

- **Keycloak** – For enterprises that need **centralized authentication with support for multiple directories.**
- **Auth0** – Recommended for **applications that require compliance** with standards like **GDPR and HIPAA.**
- **Firebase Authentication** – For developers looking for a **managed and easy-to-integrate solution.**

With its flexible and highly secure architecture, Ory is an excellent solution for applications requiring advanced identity control and robust authentication.

CHAPTER 40 – OPEN POLICY AGENT (OPA)

The security of modern applications requires **dynamic, flexible, and centralized access control**. **Open Policy Agent (OPA)** is an **open-source policy engine** designed to enable **policy definition, evaluation, and management** in a **decentralized manner**. Unlike **traditional rule-based approaches** embedded directly in application code, OPA allows **authorization logic to be decoupled** from source code, providing greater **flexibility and scalability**.

OPA is used in various scenarios, from access control in REST and GraphQL APIs to validating configurations in Kubernetes, CI/CD pipelines, and Infrastructure as Code. It utilizes a declarative policy language called Rego, allowing developers to create sophisticated rules that define who can access what and under what conditions.

Unlike solutions like Auth0 or Keycloak, which handle authentication and user sessions, OPA does not store users or authentication tokens. Instead, it acts as a policy decision engine, enabling systems to determine whether a request should be accepted or denied based on pre-configured rules.

Installation and Basic Configuration

OPA can run **locally, inside containers, or in Kubernetes environments**.

Installing OPA Locally

Download and install the OPA binary:

bash

```
curl -L -o opa https://openpolicyagent.org/downloads/latest/
opa_linux_amd64
chmod +x opa
mv opa /usr/local/bin/
```

Verify if OPA was installed correctly:

bash

```
opa version
```

The output should display the installed **OPA version.**

Running OPA as a Server

To evaluate policies **in real-time**, OPA can be started as an HTTP server:

bash

```
opa run --server
```

This starts an HTTP server **on port 8181**, ready to evaluate **policy requests.**

Key Features and Differentiators

OPA stands out from other access control solutions due to its flexibility and independence from application code.

Its main features include:

- **Real-time policy evaluation** – Allows **dynamic permission decisions.**
- **Decoupled from application code** – Access rules **do not need to be embedded in backend logic.**
- **Integration with Kubernetes, APIs, and cloud services** – Can be used to **validate REST requests** and enforce **security rules.**

- **Rego policy language** – A **declarative** language that enables **custom access rules**.
- **Distributed execution** – Can be deployed **on containers, servers, or edge computing** environments.

Use Cases and When to Choose

OPA is ideal for applications that require granular access control, allowing dynamic policies to be implemented without modifying application code.

Some common use cases include:

- **Authorization in REST and GraphQL APIs** – Evaluating permissions for **protected endpoints**.
- **Policy validation in Kubernetes** – Controlling **cluster security and configurations**.
- **Security enforcement in CI/CD pipelines** – Ensuring **compliance during deployment processes**.
- **Attribute-Based Access Control (ABAC)** – Defining **dynamic rules** based on **users, roles, and request context**.

If the application requires full user management and authentication, tools like Keycloak or Auth0 may be more suitable. OPA should be used as a complementary tool, focusing on authorization and policy evaluation.

Practical Demonstration with Code

Creating a Simple Authorization Policy

In OPA, policies are written in **Rego**. Suppose we need to **allow access only to administrators**. We can define the following policy:

rego

```
package authz

default allow = false
```

```rego
allow {
   input.user.role == "admin"
}
```

This policy sets the default permission to deny access, except for users with the "admin" role.

Evaluating the Policy in OPA

Save the policy in a file named **policy.rego**.
Evaluate an **access request**:

bash

```bash
echo '{ "user": { "role": "admin" } }' | opa eval -i - -d policy.rego "data.authz.allow"
```

If the user is an admin, the result will be true. Otherwise, it will be false.

Applying OPA to an API Endpoint

Suppose we have an API that needs to validate access permissions via OPA. We can create a policy that allows only GET requests to a protected endpoint:

rego

```rego
package api.auth

default allow = false

allow {
   input.method == "GET"
}
```

To test this policy **via the OPA server**, send an **HTTP request:**

bash

```
curl -X POST "http://localhost:8181/v1/data/api/auth/allow" \
  -H "Content-Type: application/json" \
  -d '{ "method": "GET" }'
```

If the **policy is satisfied**, the response will be { "result": true }, allowing access.

Common Errors and How to Fix Them

Error: "undefined decision" when querying policy

- **Cause:** The policy was **not properly loaded** into OPA.
- **Solution:** Ensure that the **policy.rego** file is **correct** and has been **loaded into OPA**.

Error: "false" even for authorized users

- **Cause:** The input request **does not match the expected format** in the policy.
- **Solution:** Verify the **JSON request structure** and adjust the **policy logic** accordingly.

Error: "OPA server not reachable" when accessing via API

- **Cause:** The **OPA server** may **not be running**.
- **Solution:** Start OPA using:

bash

```
opa run --server
```

before making **policy queries**.

Best Practices and Optimization

- **Keep policies modularized** – Separate rules **by context** (e.g., API, database, CI/CD).
- **Use logs and auditing** – Record **policy evaluations** for **security analysis**.

- **Integrate with Identity Providers (IdPs)** – Combine **OPA** with **Keycloak, Auth0, or other authentication services**.
- **Cache policy decisions** – To optimize performance, store **frequently accessed policy results**.

Alternatives and Competing Frameworks

- **Keycloak Authorization Services** – Provides **centralized access control** for **enterprise applications**.
- **AWS IAM Policies** – **Amazon's identity and access management** solution for **AWS services**.
- **Casbin** – A **lightweight** access control library **based on rules**.

OPA stands out as a highly flexible and scalable solution for dynamic access control in APIs, Kubernetes, and CI/CD pipelines, allowing authorization and security policies to be managed independently from application code.

FINAL CONCLUSION

Web development and API creation have evolved significantly in recent years, demanding increasingly robust, flexible, and efficient tools. Throughout this book, we have explored **40 essential frameworks**, covering **frontend, backend, APIs, full-stack development, serverless, and security**, providing a comprehensive overview of the most widely used technologies today.

The first module covered **frontend frameworks**, fundamental for building modern and responsive interfaces. **React, Vue.js, and Angular** lead the industry, offering reusable components and support for scalable applications. Emerging technologies such as **Svelte, Solid.js, Next.js, and Nuxt.js** introduced innovative approaches, standing out in terms of performance and user experience optimization.

In the **backend module**, we analyzed frameworks that support **business logic and data processing**. **Express.js, NestJS, and Fastify** dominated the discussion in the **Node.js ecosystem**, while **Django and Flask** established themselves as powerful options for **Python development**. In the **Java ecosystem**, **Spring Boot and Micronaut** were explored for their ability to create **robust applications**. Additionally, **Ruby on Rails** demonstrated its characteristic **productivity**, while **Fiber and Laravel** presented **efficient solutions for Go and PHP**, respectively.

The **third module focused on system integration**, where we explored **frameworks for APIs and GraphQL**. **Apollo GraphQL, Hasura, and GraphQL Yoga** demonstrated how to make **data queries more flexible and efficient**. Meanwhile, **tRPC,**

LoopBack, FastAPI, and Hapi.js expanded the possibilities for **building RESTful APIs**, combining **performance and ease of use.**

Full-stack frameworks were covered in the fourth module, highlighting **technologies that unify frontend and backend. RedwoodJS and Blitz.js** introduced **modern approaches based on React**, while **AdonisJS and Meteor** expanded **JavaScript's role** in full application development. **Strapi and Remix** showcased how to **simplify the creation of dynamic and interactive applications.**

In the **fifth module, we explored technologies transforming cloud application deployment.** The **Serverless Framework** simplified **serverless function execution**, while **Vercel and Netlify** stood out in **optimizing frontend applications.** Additionally, **AWS Amplify** provided a **comprehensive set of tools for AWS-based applications**, and **Deno Deploy** introduced a **new paradigm for edge computing execution.**

Security was the central theme of the **final module**, essential for **data protection and access control** in web applications. **Auth.js, Keycloak, and Supabase Auth** demonstrated **robust authentication and identity management solutions. Ory and Open Policy Agent (OPA)** introduced **advanced access control strategies**, reinforcing the **importance of security** in modern projects.

The evolution of **web development and APIs** continues at a rapid pace, and staying up to date with **the best tools is essential to standing out** in the industry. Each framework presented here was chosen for its **impact and relevance**, allowing **developers, software architects, and engineers** to make **more strategic decisions** when selecting **technologies for their projects.**

Continuous learning and hands-on experimentation are essential for **deepening knowledge and mastering each tool. Technology is constantly changing**, and the **differentiator of**

a professional lies in their ability to adapt and innovate. The **path to excellence in development** requires **constant practice and an ongoing pursuit of improvement**.

We appreciate your journey with us throughout this book. We hope this content has added **knowledge and provided a clear perspective** on the **main frameworks** in the **web development and API ecosystem**. May this material serve as a **solid foundation** to advance your **career and projects in the world of technology**.

Sincerely,
Diego Rodrigues & Team!